interpretations
Volume 2

by joji locatelli and veera välimäki

photographs by jonna jolkin

POM POM PRESS
LONDON

Published in 2016 by the Pom Pom Press

Text © 2016 Joji Locatelli & Veera Välimäki

Photographs © 2016 Jonna Jolkin

All rights reserved. No portion of this book may be reproduced or transmitted in any form or by any means, mechanical, electronic, photocopying, recording, or otherwise, without written permission of the publisher.

ISBN: 978-0-9934866-2-3

A catalogue record for this book is available from the British Library.

Editors: Meghan Fernandes & Lydia Gluck

Associate Editor: Amy Collins

Printed in the UK by Park Communications

POM POM PRESS

B203 Lighthouse Space
89A Shacklewell Lane
London E8 2EB
United Kingdom
pompommag.com

contents

pure

    true cardigan   page 12
    float pullover   page 18

grace

    falling stole   page 28
    salt and sand   page 34

unimaginable

    adventurous   page 44
    fly forward   page 52

focus

    ley lines shawl   page 60
    true friend   page 66

quiet

    serenity sweater   page 76
    above the horizon   page 82

charm

    petites bulles   page 90
    state of mind   page 94

foreword

Printed out before you is a river of moments, thoughts and feelings flowing together into new creative designs. Two friends from opposite sides of the world combining our love of our countries and beautiful knitwear. Little did we know that our first adventure, Interpretations, would mark the beginning of an entirely new approach to designing as our dream project continued.

Influencing each other, challenging and igniting one another, this entire adventure has been about becoming something new, going outside of your reality and visiting someone else's for a while. Letting yourself be overcome by a new country. Trusting in one another, holding hands during a new creative approach. All these ideas were born into Interpretations 2.

As we did with the first collection, we chose six themes, six words with a strong meaning for us: grace, focus, charm, quiet, pure and unimaginable. There are two designs for each theme, and they show our personal take on each of these words.

When all the designs were finished, we chose Finland as the location for our photo-shoot, which was as magical as the one in Argentina. The windy shores of Hanko were exactly the place we had dreamed for our knits to glow, letting show the contrasts and similarities of our origins. Southern Finland was misty and mesmerizing, a place never to be forgotten.

This time, knowing each other very well, and knowing what we were doing, the process flowed, was natural and relaxed, moving of its own will, making its own life. It was a journey to be enjoyed from start to finish. We hope you enjoy it too!

happy knitting,
joji and veera

pure

Thick green moss creeps its way through the rocks on the path before me. The only sounds to be heard are seagulls, far in the horizon, as they lift off from the mist covered water. A deep breath reveals cold soil and salty waters. I want to breathe in, again and again, to keep it coming. I stop and see it, a warm rock to perch on so I can take in this moment; it is undiluted and simple, blissful. I feel at peace and in harmony with this scene around me. Everything seems to be in its place, right where it is supposed to be. This to me feels pure.

Purity can be seen in many ways. For knitters there is a little bit of purity in the act of knitting.

Individually we have crafted these patterns to carefully represent the mood we aspire to achieve. Together we strive to always fashion our knits in the most down to earth way, these are designs with the sweetest intentions at their core.

Designed purely, from the bottom of our hearts.

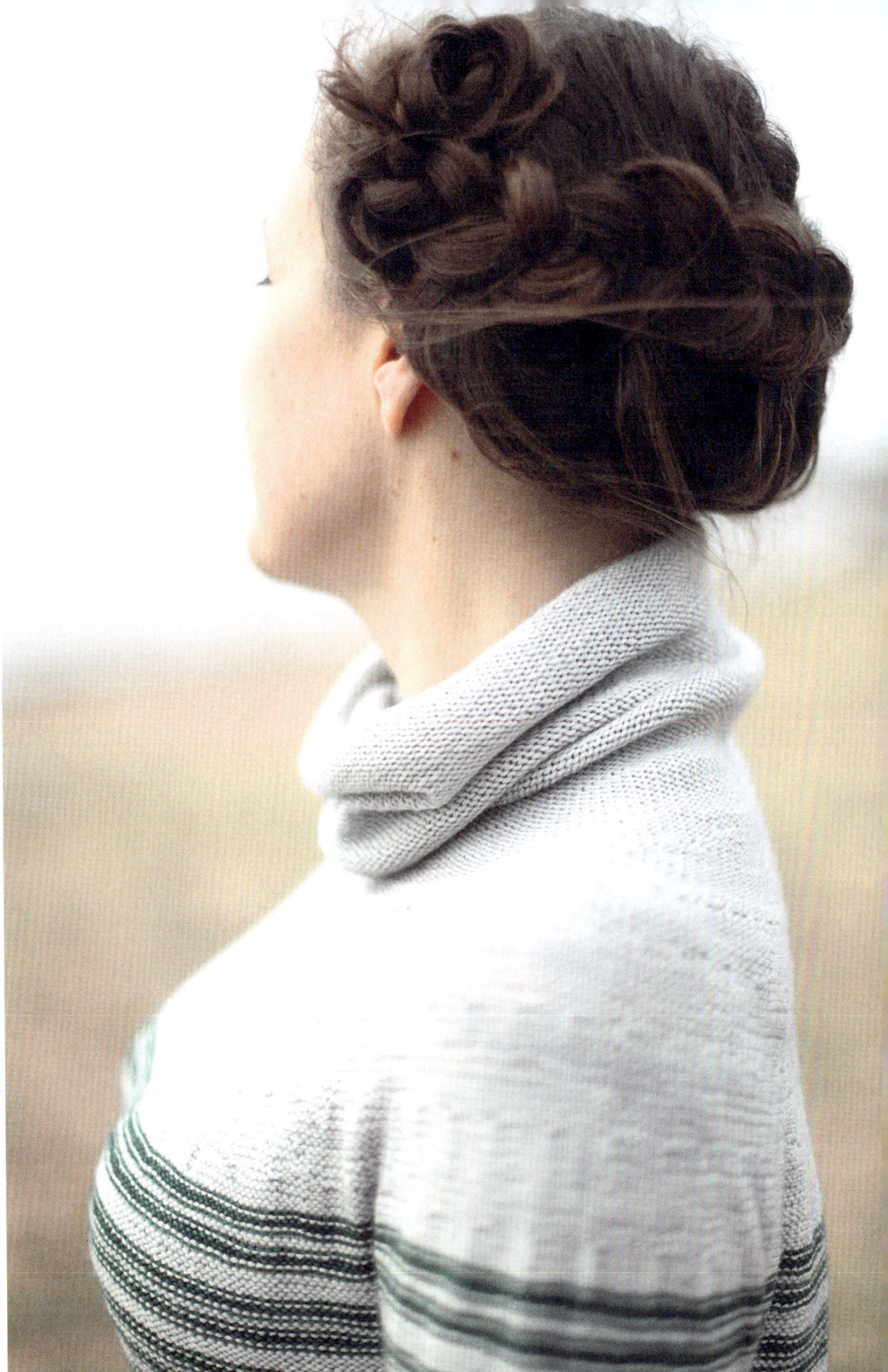

pure

true cardigan

float pullover

true

by joji locatelli

Pure, untouched beauty lies in the heart of this coat. Sometimes it is good to have a coat that feels like a friend, that makes you feel always comfortable... Almost like a big hug. This design is about the simplicity of knitting something that makes you happy without needing anything added. Just a wonderful cardigan, pure and simple.

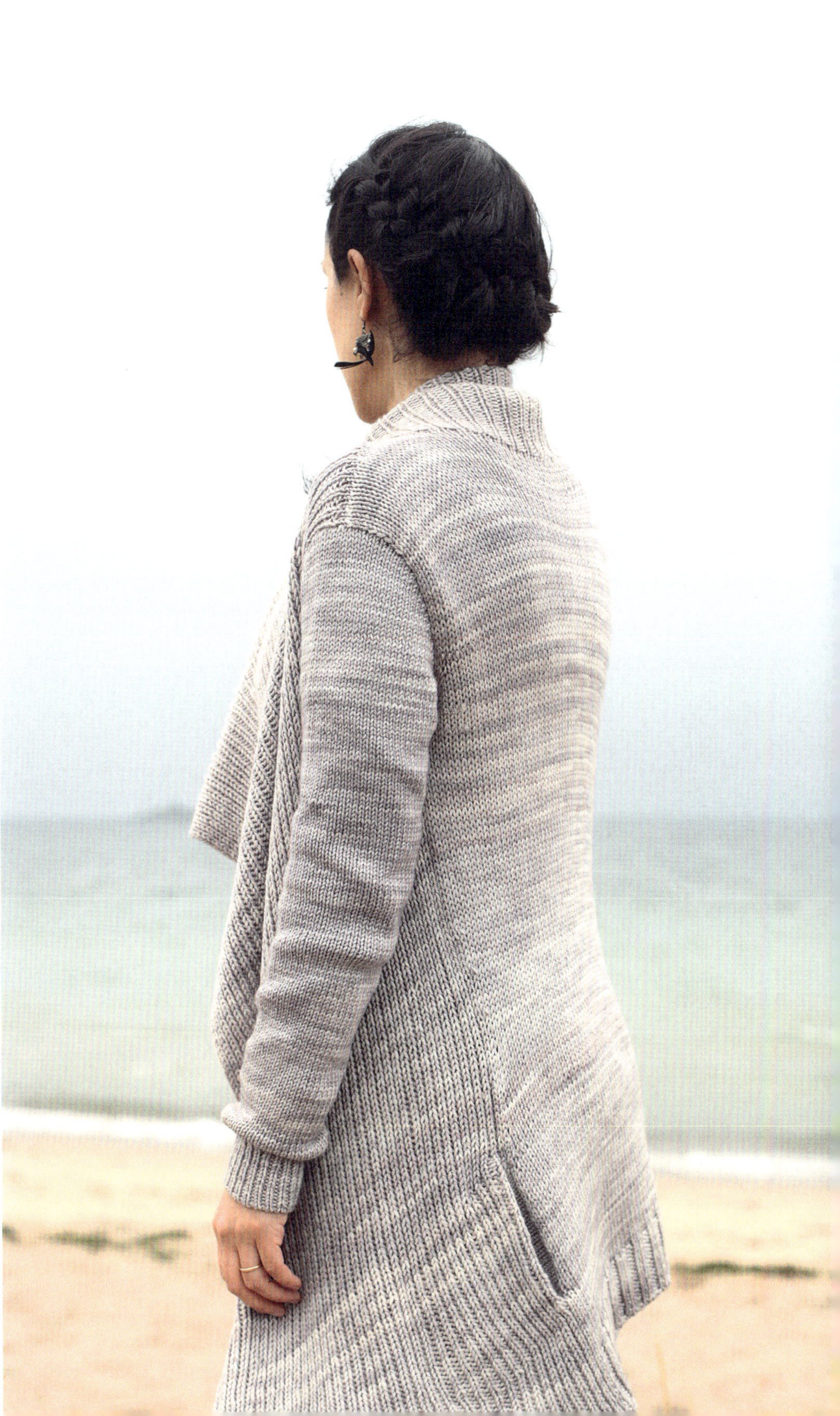

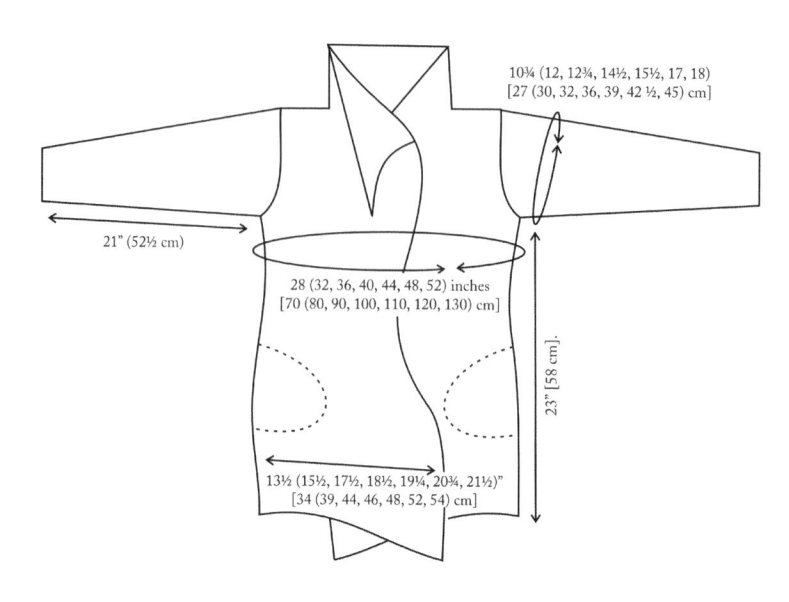

true

Sizes

XS (S, M, L, XL, XXL, 3XL). Shown in size M.

Finished bust circumference (according to back measurement): 28 (32, 36, 40, 44, 48, 52)" [70 (80, 90, 100, 110, 120, 130) cm]. *Note: This sweater is intended to be worn open, so to get the correct size, measure across your back from underarm to underarm; then double that measurement and choose the size above which is closest to that number. Note: See more detailed finished measurements below in schematics picture or written on page 17.*

Materials

Yarn: 7 (7, 8, 8, 9, 9, 10) skeins of DK Twist by Madelinetosh (100% merino, 250 yd [229 m] - 100 g). Approx 1550 (1650, 1850, 1950, 2100, 2200, 2350) yd [1417 (1509, 1692, 1783, 1920, 2200, 2012) m] of DK weight yarn. The sample was knit in size M using colorway Smokestack.

Needles: US 7 (4.5 mm) and US 6 (4 mm) circular needles.

Other: Stitch markers, stitch holders, waste yarn, row counter (optional).

Gauge

16.5 st and 28 rows = 4", on US 7 (4.5 mm) needles, in Stockinette stitch, after blocking.

Finished Measurements

10¾ (12, 12¾, 14½, 15½, 17, 18)
[27 (30, 32, 36, 39, 42 ½, 45) cm]

21" (52½ cm)

28 (32, 36, 40, 44, 48, 52) inches
[70 (80, 90, 100, 110, 120, 130) cm]

23" [58 cm]

13½ (15½, 17½, 18½, 19¼, 20¾, 21½)"
[34 (39, 44, 46, 48, 52, 54) cm]

true

Collar and Back

With larger needles, CO 121 (133, 151, 155, 161, 173, 179) st using the method of your preference (I used a tubular CO on my sample).

Work 8" (20 cm) in p1, k1 ribbing, starting and ending the RS rows with p1, and finishing on a WS row.

Next row (RS): Work 45 (51, 59, 61, 63, 69, 71) st in pattern and put them on hold. We will call these sts "Left front sts". Work 31 (31, 33, 33, 35, 35, 37) st in pattern, and place the remaining 45 (51, 59, 61, 63, 69, 71) st on a separate holder. We will call these sts "Right front sts". You should have only 31 (31, 33, 33, 35, 35, 37) st left on your needles.

Next row (WS): CO 12 (14, 17, 19, 20, 23, 24) st (Right Shoulder st), p18 (20, 23, 25, 26, 29, 30), (p2tog, p6) 3 times, p to end of row.

Next row (RS): CO 12 (14, 17, 19, 20, 23, 25) st (Left Shoulder st), knit to end of row. You should have 52 (56, 64, 68, 72, 78, 82) st on the needles.

Next row (WS): Purl to end of row.

Continue working in Stockinette st until your piece measures 5½, 6, 6½ (6¾, 7, 7¼, 7¼)" [14 (15, 16, 16½, 17½, 18, 18) cm] from your Shoulder st CO, ending with a WS row.

Next row (RS): K2, m1R, k to 2 st from end, m1L, k2.

Next row (WS): Purl all st.

Repeat the last 2 rows 2 (2, 2, 3, 4, 5, 7) more times. *You should have 58 (62, 70, 76, 82, 90, 98) st.*

Break yarn and put all st on hold

Right front

With larger needles, starting at the outer edge, pick up and knit 17 (19, 21, 21, 23, 25, 27) st along the Right Shoulder st (the gauge in Stockinette st and ribbing is not the same, so you will have to pick up more stitches than there are in the back - Pick up the last one of these st from the gap between these st and the st you had on hold). Place the Right Front st onto the left needle and work them in pattern to the end of row. *You should have 62 (70, 80, 82, 86, 94, 98) st on the needles.*

Next row (WS): (K1, p1) to end.

Continue working in k1, p1 ribbing, until your work measures 5¼, 5¾, 6¼, 6¼, 6¾, 7, 7)" [13½ (14½, 15½, 16, 17, 17½, 17½) cm] from the point where you picked up your stitches, ending with a WS row.

Next row (RS): K1, p1, m1p, (k1, p1) to end of row.

Next row: Work in patt to end.

Next row: K1, p1, m1R, p1, (k1, p1) to end.

Next row: Work in patt to end.

Repeat the last 4 rows 1 (1, 1, 1, 2, 2, 3) more times. *Your front should have 66 (74, 84, 86, 92, 100, 106) st.*

Break yarn and put all st on hold.

15

left front

With larger needles, starting at the neck edge, pick up and knit 17 (19, 21, 21, 23, 25, 27) st along the Left Shoulder st (pick up the first of these from the gap between these st and the st you had on hold). Turn work.

Next row (WS): P17 (19, 21, 21, 23, 25, 27); place the Left Front st you had on hold onto the left needle and work them in pattern to the end of the row. *You should have 62 (70, 80, 82, 86, 94, 98) st on the needles.*

Next row (RS): (P1, k1) to end.

Continue working in p1, k1 ribbing until your work measures 5¼, 5¾, 6¼, 6¼, 6¾, 7, 7)" [13½ (14½, 15½, 16, 17, 17½, 17½) cm] from the point where you picked up your st, ending with a WS row.

Next row (RS): (P1, k1) to 2 st from end, m1p, p1, k1.

Next row: Work in patt to end.

Next row: (P1, k1) to 3 st from end, p1, m1L, p1, k1.

Next row: Work in patt to end.

Repeat the last 4 rows 1 (1, 1, 1, 2, 2, 3) more times. Do not break yarn. *Your front should have 66 (74, 84, 86, 92, 100, 106) st.*

Join all pieces

Work all Left Front st in pattern, CO 0 (2, 2, 3, 4, 5, 5), pm, CO 0 (2, 2, 3, 4, 5, 5); place the held st for the back onto the needles and knit them, CO 0 (2, 2, 3, 4, 5, 5) pm, CO 0 (2, 2, 3, 4, 5, 5); place the held st for the Right Front onto the needles and work in patt to end of row.

You should now have 190 (218, 246, 260, 282, 310, 330) st; 58 (66, 74, 82, 90, 100, 108) st for the back and 66 (76, 86, 89, 96, 105, 111) st for each front.

Next row (WS): Work in 1x1 ribbing to m, sm, p to next m, work in 1x1 ribbing to end.

Nex row (RS): Work in 1x1 ribbing to m, sm, k to next m, work in 1x1 ribbing to end.

Continue working in the established pattern until piece measures 6" (15 cm) from your armhole. Start waist shaping.

Next row (RS) - Waist decrease row: Work in patt to m, sm, k1, ssk, work in patt to 3 st before next m, k2tog, k1, sm, work in patt to end.

Continue working in pattern and repeat the *waist decrease row* every 6 rows, twice more.

On the 6th foll row after your last decrease row, start increases:

Next row (RS) - Waist increase row: Work in patt to m, sm, k2, m1R, k to 2 st before next m, m1L, k2, sm, work in patt to end of row.

Continue working in pattern and repeat the *waist increase row* every 6 rows 3 more times.

At the same time, when work measures 12¾" (32 cm) from the armhole, divide for pocket openings, starting on the foll WS row.

Next WS row: Work in patt to m, remove m, turn work.

Work back and forth in patt over the Right Front st only, for 26 more rows. Break yarn and put these st on hold.

Rejoin yarn to begin a WS row over the back st.

Next row (WS): Purl to marker, remove m, turn work.

Work back and forth in Stockinette st over the Back st only, for 26 more rows (remember to work the last body increase row here). Break yarn and put these st on hold.

Rejoin yarn to begin a WS row over the Left Front st.

Work 27 rows in pattern.

Next row (RS): Work to end of row in patt, pm, place the held st from the back on the needles and knit them, pm, place the held st from the Right Front on the needles and work in patt to end of row.

Continue working in pattern until your work measures 20" (50 cm) from the armhole, ending with a WS row.

Next row (RS):

XS, S, M, L, XL: Work in patt to m, sm, k2, m1p, p1, k2, (p2, k2) from 3 st from m, m1p, p1, k2.

XXL, XXXL: Work in patt to m, sm, k2 (p2, k2) to m, sm, work in patt to end.

Next row (WS) - all sizes: Work in patt to m, sm, p2 (k2, p2) to m, sm work in patt to end.

Next row (RS): Work in patt to m, sm, k2 (p2, k2) to m, sm, work in patt to end.

Repeat the last 2 rows 8 more times. Bind off all st loosely in pattern.

Pockets

With smaller needles, with the RS facing you and starting at the bottom corner of the pocket, pick up and knit 24 st along one of the sides of the pocket opening, pm, and pick up 24 st along the other. Place marker to start working in the round. Knit 1 round.

Next round - Shifting round: K1, m1R, k to 3 st from m, k2tog, k1, sm, k1, ssk, k to 1 st from end, m1L, k1.

Continue working in Stockinette st repeating the *shifting round* every 2 rounds 3 times, and every 4 rounds 3 more times. Work straight in Stockinette until your pocket measures 5" (12½ cm) from the point where you picked up your stitches.

Next round - Decrease round: K1, ssk, k to 3 st from m, k2tog, k1, sm, k1, ssk, k to 3 st from end, k2tog, k1.

Continue in pattern working a *decrease round* every 2 rounds twice more.

Divide the stitches into 2 halves (half on one needle and half on another). Turn the pocket inside out (with the WS facing out) and join the top of the pocket using a 3-needle-BO.

Repeat for the other pocket.

Sleeves

With US 7 (4.5 mm) needles and starting at the bottom of the armhole, pick up and knit 48 (54, 58, 64, 70, 76, 82) stitches evenly distributed around the armhole opening. Place a marker at the beginning of the round.

Sleeve Cap

Row 1: Knit 32 (36, 38, 42, 46, 50, 54), W&T.
Row 2: Purl 16 (18, 18, 20, 22, 24, 26), W&T.
Row 3: Knit to wrapped stitch, knit wrap together with wrapped stitch, W&T.
Row 4: Purl to wrapped stitch, purl wrap together with wrapped stitch, W&T.

Repeat *rows 3 and 4* until only 4 stitches remain un-worked at each side of the marker.

Next row: Knit to last wrapped stitch, knit wrap together with wrapped stitch, knit to the end of round.

Start knitting in Stockinette stitch in the round. On the 14th (12th, 12th, 8th, 7th, 6th, 5th) round after the sleeve cap is finished, knit to 2 st before marker, ssk, sm, k2tog (2 stitches decreased).

Continue working in Stockinette stitch in the round repeating the *decrease round* every 16 (12, 12, 10, 9, 8, 7) rounds, 4 (6, 7, 8, 9, 11, 12) more times.

38 (40, 42, 46, 50, 52, 56) st remain.

Continue working in pattern until your sleeve measures 18" (45 cm) measured from the bottom of the armhole.

Switch to US 6 (4 mm) needles and start cuff.

Next round: (K1, p1) to end of round.

Work in the established ribbing for 3" (7½ cm), and on the foll round BO all st loosely in pattern.

Finishing

Block garment to measurements and weave in ends.

You might want to secure the inside of the pocket into place with a few stitches to prevent it from hanging backwards.

Finished Measurements

Bust circumference (according to back measurement): 28 (32, 36, 40, 44, 48, 52)" [70 (80, 90, 100, 110, 120, 130) cm]. *Note: This sweater is intended to be worn open, so to get the correct size, measure across your back from underarm to underarm; then double that measurement and choose the size above which is closest to that number.*

Front Flap width: 13½ (15½, 17½, 18½, 19¼, 20¾, 21½)" [34 (39, 44, 46, 48, 52, 54) cm]

Upper arm circumference: 10¾ (12, 12¾, 14½, 15½, 17, 18) [27 (30, 32, 36, 39, 42 ½, 45) cm].

Sleeve length from underarm to cuff: 21" (52½ cm).

Length from underarm to hem: 23" [58 cm].

float

by veera välimäki

Float is an easy sweater, pure in its simplicity but highly wearable and fun with the rhythmic stripes. Worked seamlessly from top down with a round yoke, this piece is a true classic. Choose your colors carefully and see where the stripes lead.

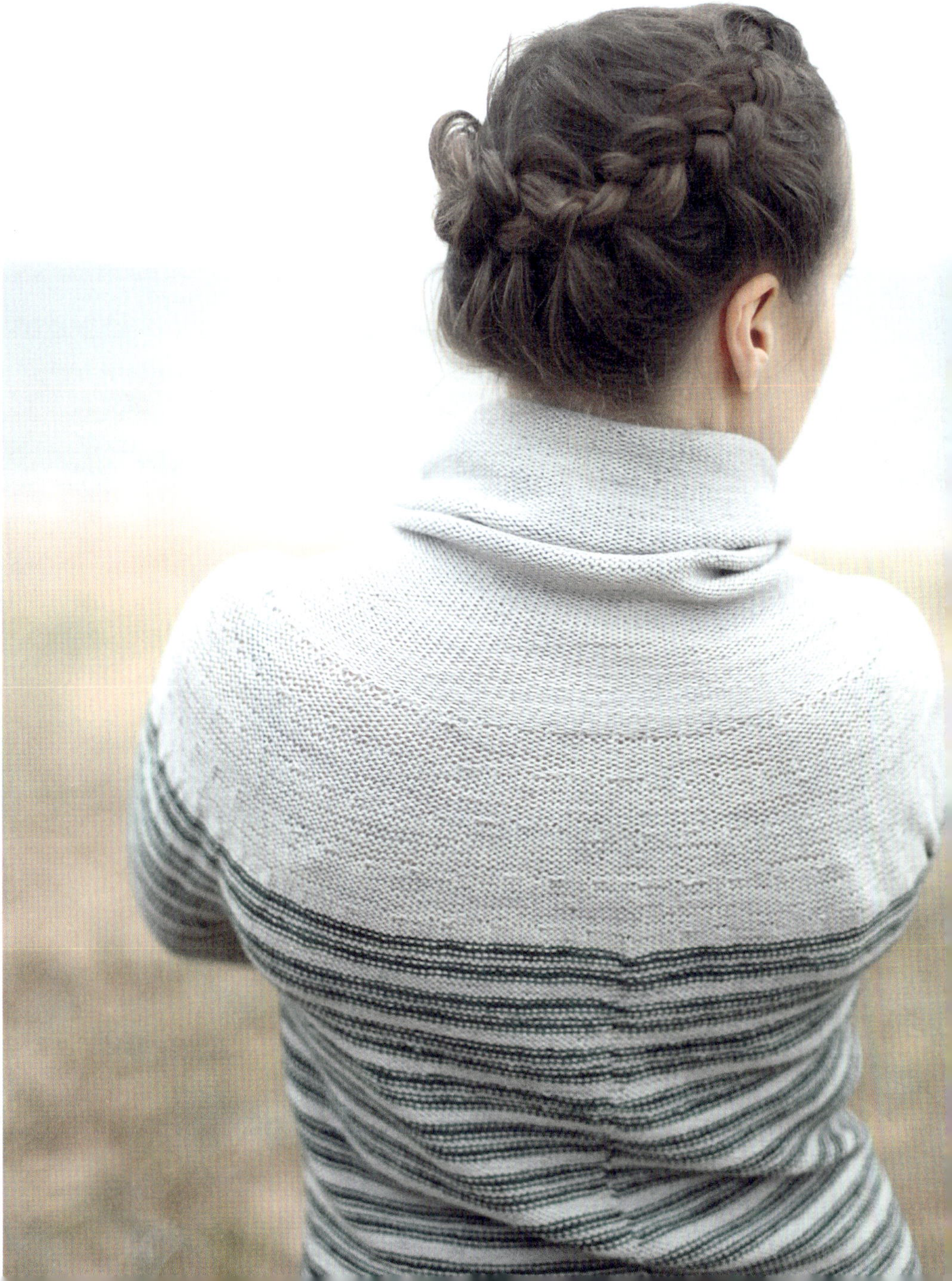

float

Sizes

XS (S, M, L, XL, XXL), shown in size S.

Finished chest circumference: 30 (34, 38, 42, 46, 50)" [75 (85, 95, 105, 115, 125) cm]. Choose a size with a small amount of positive ease.

Materials

Yarn: 4 (4, 5, 5, 6, 6) skeins of Uncommon Everyday by The Uncommon Thread (100% merino; 440 yd [402 m] - 100 g). Approx. 1540 (1690, 1880, 2110, 2320, 2470) yd [1400 (1550, 1720, 1930, 2120, 2260) m] of fingering weight yarn; 3 (3, 4, 4, 5, 5) skeins of MC and one skein of CC. The sample was knit in colorways Breath (MC, grey) and Dartmoor (CC, green).

Needles: US 2½ [3 mm] circular needle, 24" [60 cm] long or longer, and dpns. Adjust needle size if necessary to obtain the correct gauge.

Other: Stitch markers, stitch holders / waste yarn, tapestry needle and blocking aids.

Gauge

28 stitches and 36 rows = 4" [10 cm] in Stockinette stitch.

Finished Measurements

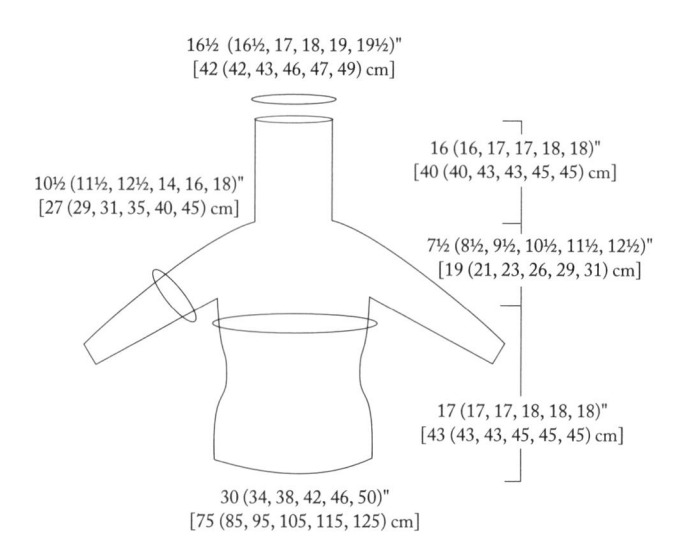

16½ (16½, 17, 18, 19, 19½)"
[42 (42, 43, 46, 47, 49) cm]

16 (16, 17, 17, 18, 18)"
[40 (40, 43, 43, 45, 45) cm]

10½ (11½, 12½, 14, 16, 18)"
[27 (29, 31, 35, 40, 45) cm]

7½ (8½, 9½, 10½, 11½, 12½)"
[19 (21, 23, 26, 29, 31) cm]

17 (17, 17, 18, 18, 18)"
[43 (43, 43, 45, 45, 45) cm]

30 (34, 38, 42, 46, 50)"
[75 (85, 95, 105, 115, 125) cm]

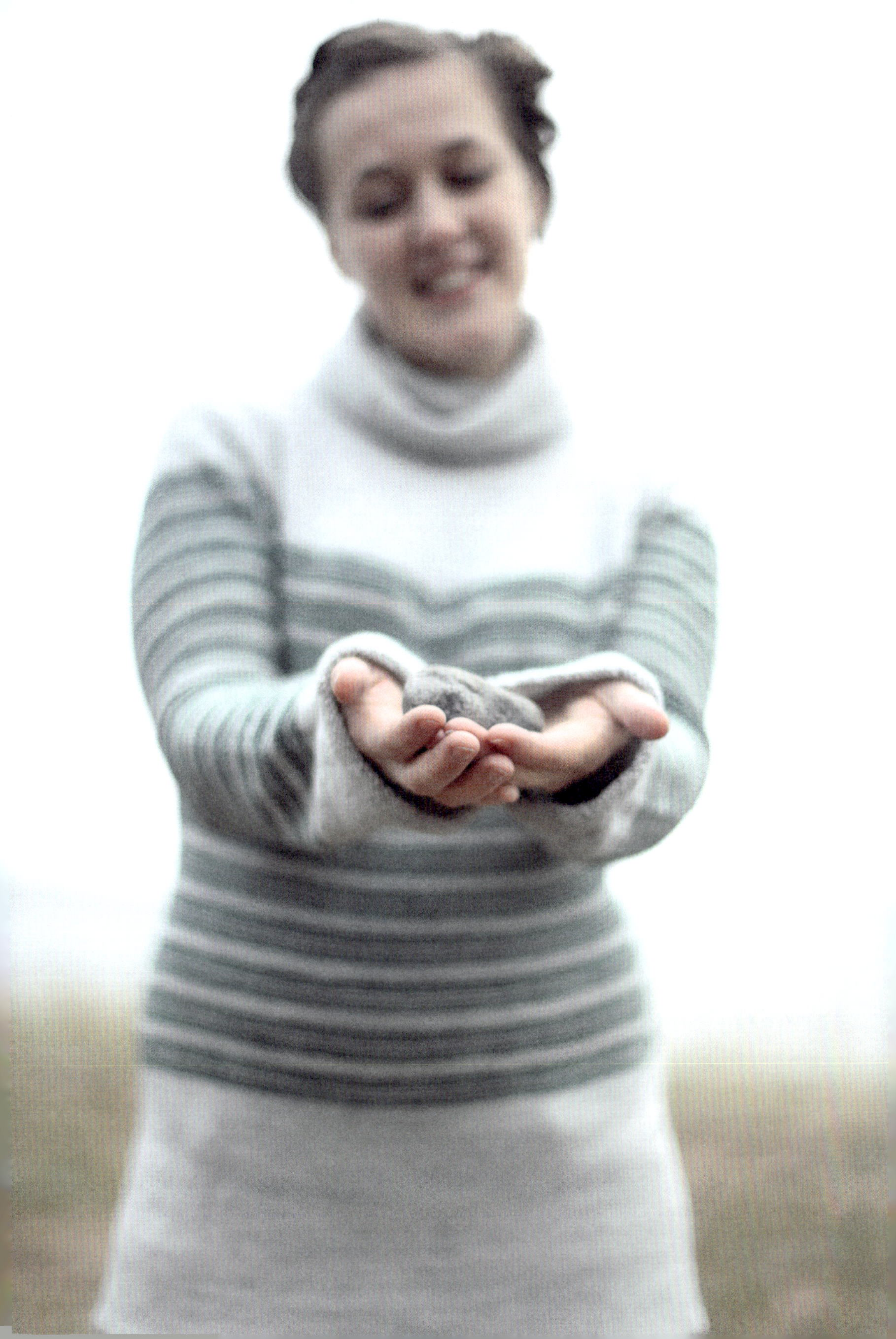

float

Note: the sweater will be worked from inside out (Stockinette side on top, knitting not purling), to make it easier to do. Make sure you keep the yarn changes and all yarn ends on that Stockinette side as well. If you prefer to work reverse Stockinette stitch instead of Stockinette, you can easily work the pattern with right side up as well, just switch Stockinette with reverse Stockinette. Twist MC and CC yarns at color changes to avoid any holes or gaps.

Collar

Using main color (MC) and circular needle, CO 116 (116, 120, 128, 132, 136) sts. Carefully join in round, not twisting your stitches, and pm for beginning of round. *Note: if you have trouble working the collar on circular needle, you can CO using dpns as well or use magic loop technique with circular needle. Change to circular needle when necessary.*

Work 17" [43 cm] in Stockinette stitch.

Yoke

Begin short rows for neck shaping:

Row 1 (St st side): Knit 20 (20, 22, 22, 24, 26), turn work.

Row 2 (rev St st side): Yo, purl to marker, sm, purl 20 (20, 22, 22, 24, 26), turn work.

Row 3 (St st side): Yo, knit to marker, sm, knit to previous yo, ssk the yarn over with the next stitch (the yo remains visible on St st side), k2, turn work.

Row 4 (rev St st side): Yo, purl to marker, sm, purl to previous yo, p2tog the yarn over with the next stitch (the yo remains visible on St st side), p2, turn work.

Repeat **rows 3 and 4** four times more. Work to end of round: yo, knit to marker. Continue working St st in the round and pick up the two remaining yarn overs on first round: knit to yo, ssk the yo together with the next stitch, knit until one stitch before last yo remains, k2tog the next stitch with the yo, k to end.

Begin yoke increases

All sizes:

Increase round 1 (St st side): Sm, *k1, k1fb; repeat from * to end of round. [*174 (174, 180, 192, 198, 204) sts*].

Work 1" [2.5 cm] in St st.

Increase round 2 (St st side): Sm, *k2, k1fb; repeat from * to end of round. [*232 (232, 240, 256, 264, 272) sts*].

Work 1" [2.5 cm] in St st.

Increase round 3 (St st side): Sm, *k3, k1fb; repeat from * to end of round. [*290 (290, 300, 320, 330, 340) sts*].

Work 1" [2.5 cm] in St st.

Increase round 4 (St st side): Sm, *k4, k1fb; repeat from * to end of round. [*348 (348, 360, 384, 396, 408) sts*].

Work 1" [2.5 cm] in St st.

Sizes M, L, XL and XXL only:

Increase round 5 (St st side): Sm, *k5, k1fb; repeat from * to end of round. [*348 (348, 420, 448, 462, 476) sts*].

Work 1" [2.5 cm] in St st.

Sizes XL and XXL only:

Increase round 6 (St st side): Sm, *k6, k1fb; repeat from * to end of round. [*348 (348, 420, 448, 528, 544) sts*].

Work 1" [2.5 cm] in St st.

All sizes:

Begin striping – continue working in St st and work two rounds in CC, two rounds in MC, two rounds in CC and four rounds in MC. Continue striping, working in St st until the yoke measures 7½ (8½, 9½, 10½, 11½, 12½)" [19 (21, 23, 26, 29, 31) cm] from short rows.

Divide for body and sleeves

Next row (RS): Slip marker, knit 51 (53, 64, 68, 78, 80) stitches, place the next 71 (67, 82, 87, 107, 111) stitches on holder for sleeve, CO 1 (6, 3, 5, 2, 7) stitches using backwards-loop cast-on, pm for side, CO 1 (6, 2, 5, 2, 7) stitches using backwards-loop cast-on, knit 103 (107, 128, 137, 157, 161) stitches, place the next 71 (67, 82, 87, 107, 111) stitches on holder for sleeve, CO 1 (6, 3, 5, 2, 7) stitches using backwards-loop cast-on, pm for side, CO 1 (6, 2, 5, 2, 7) stitches using backwards-loop cast-on, knit to end.

You have 71 (67, 82, 87, 107, 111) stitches on each holder for sleeves and 210 (238, 266, 294, 322, 350) stitches on needle for the body.

Body

Continue striping in St st (two rounds in CC, two rounds in MC, two rounds in CC and four rounds in MC). When body measures 3" [8 cm] from underarm begin waist decreases.

Decrease round (St st side, keep striping continuous): *Knit until 6 stitches before marker remain, k2tog, k4, sm, k4, ssk; repeat once from *, knit to end.

Repeat the *decrease round* every 4th round 3 (3, 4, 4, 4, 4) more times [*194 (222, 246, 274, 302, 330) stitches*]. Work 2" [5 cm] striping in St st. Begin waist increases.

Increase round (St st side, keep striping continuous): *Knit until 5 stitches before marker remain, m1R, k5, sm, k5, m1L; repeat once from *, knit to end.

Repeat the *increase round* every 4th round 3 (3, 4, 4, 4, 4) more times [*210 (238, 266, 294, 322, 350) stitches*]. Work one more sequence of the striping. Continue with MC only and work in St st until the body measures 17 (17, 17, 18, 18, 18)" [43 (43, 43, 45, 45, 45) cm] from underarm. BO stitches loosely on next round.

Sleeves

Place the held stitches on dpns (or on circular needle using magic loop technique). Join the correct yarn (keeping the striping continuous, MC or CC) to middle of CO underarm stitches and pick up and knit 1 (6, 3, 6, 3, 8) stitches, work the previously held stitches and pick up and knit 2 (7, 3, 6, 3, 7) stitches to end of round. Place marker for beginning of round and join. *74 (80, 88, 99, 113, 126) stitches on needle.*

Continue striping in St st (two rounds in CC, two rounds in MC, two rounds in CC and four rounds in MC). When sleeve measures 2" [5 cm] from underarm begin decreases.

Decrease round (St st side, keep striping continuous): k2, ssk, k until 4 stitches remain, k2tog, k2.

Repeat the *decrease round* every 2" [5 cm] 4 (4, 4, 5, 5, 5) more times [*64 (70, 78, 87, 101, 114) stitches*]. Work one more sequence of the striping after the last decrease, then continue with MC only.

Work in St st until the sleeve measures 20" [50 cm] from underarm. BO stitches loosely on next round.

Finishing

Turn the sweater inside-out as you have been working from the knit side, weave in ends and block garment to finished measurements.

grace

The sound of ocean, making its way back and forth, waves glistening in your ears. The sound of ocean can feel like a grace in itself. Being subtle and strong, being kind and solid, all at the same time. Like the sea shapes the coast, a bit more with every wave, each stitch sculpts the essence of these designs.

In these designs you can see the suppleness of movement, just like the ocean flows. You can find small details making them poised and full of bliss. The details will keep the process of knitting smooth as the magic is right below the surface, the grace.

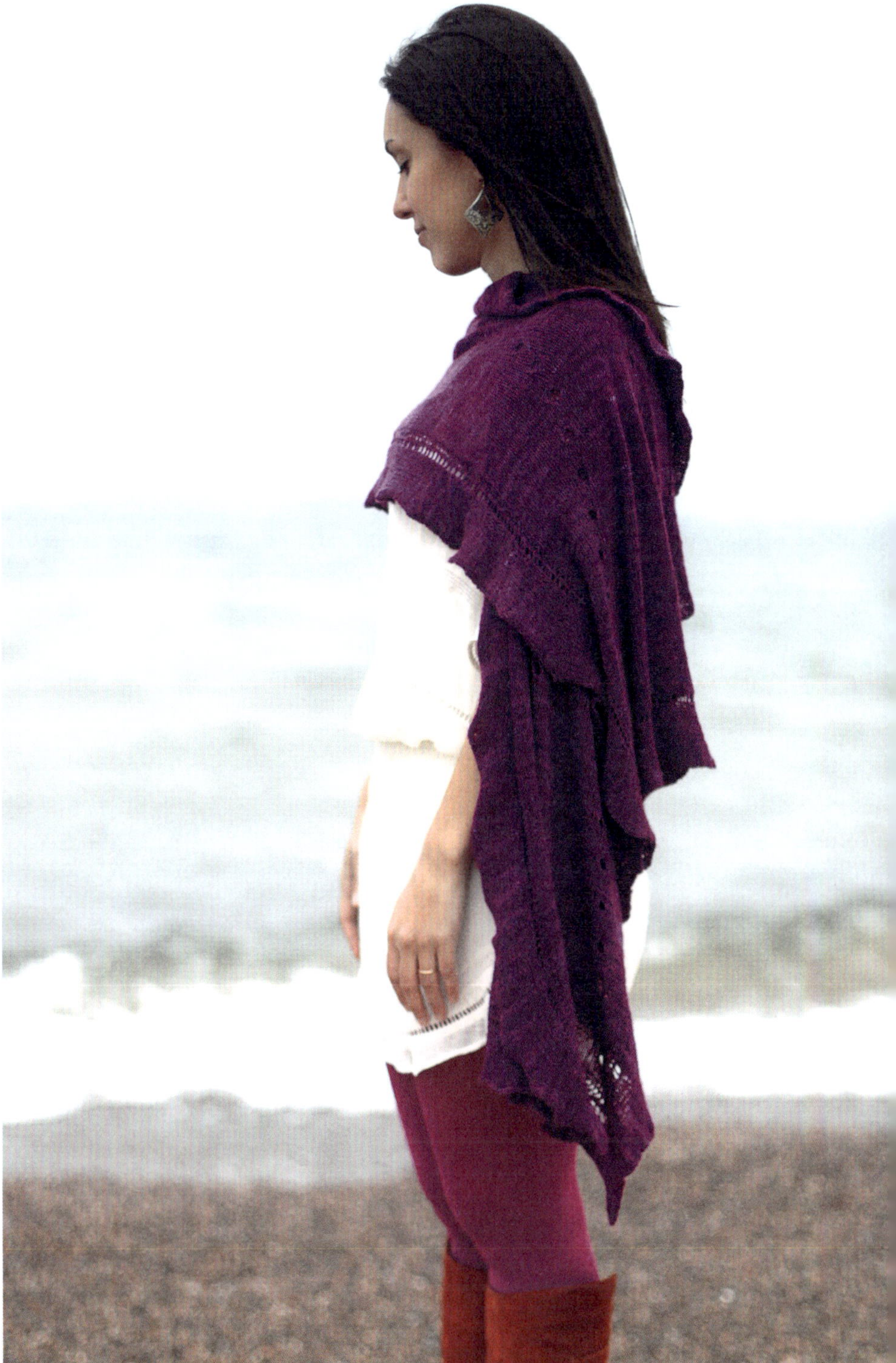

grace

falling stole

salt and sand top

falling

by joji locatelli

Everything about this design makes me think of Grace: the sweetly airy fabric, the soft fibers it was made with, the striking beauty of its color, the subtle shaping of the edge that lets the wind move its wings.

Fall in love with this elegant stole and its flowing curves. Knitted with a lightweight yarn at a very open gauge, its movement will charm you every time you wear it.

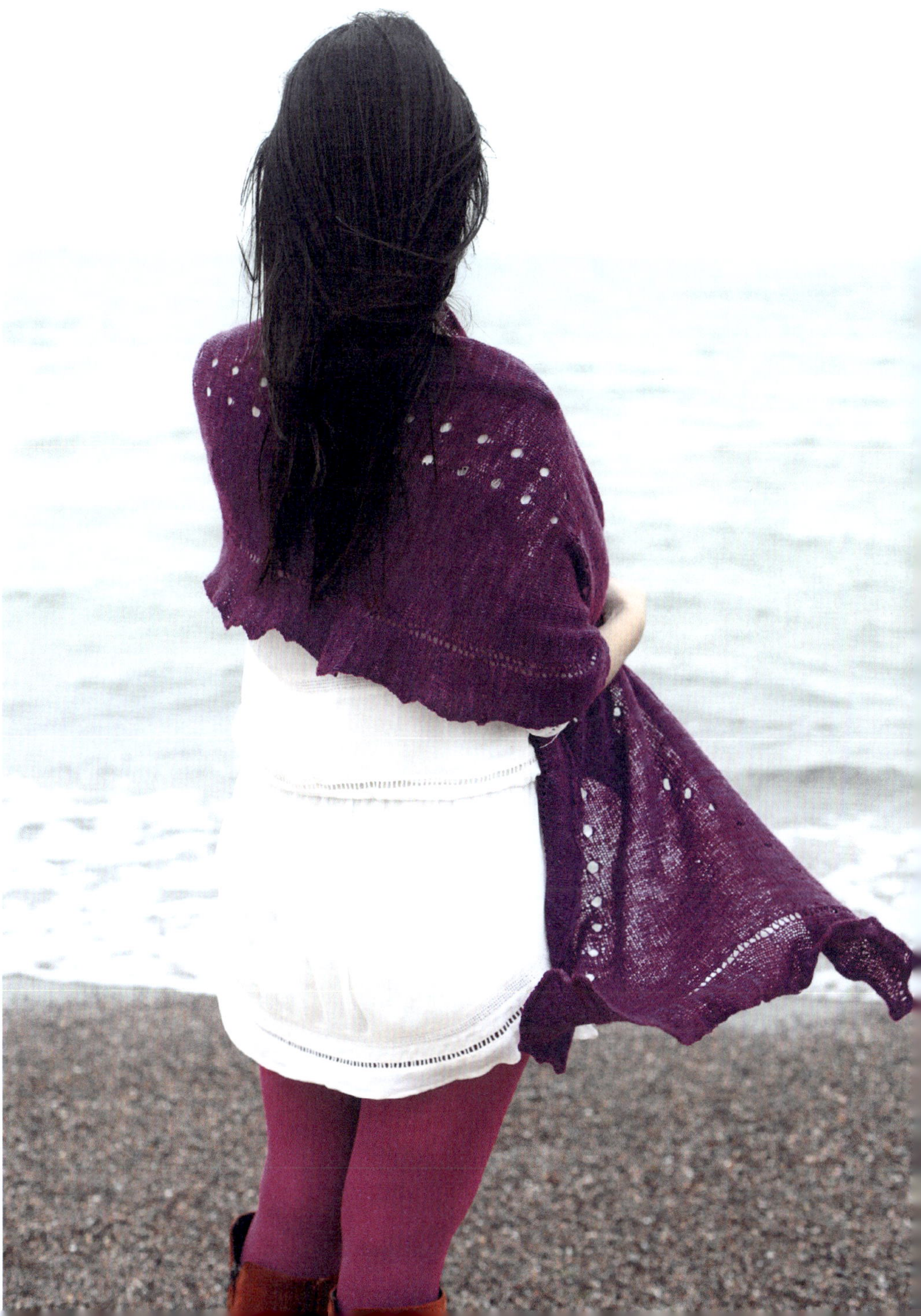

falling

Sizes

One size.

Finished measurements: Approx. 72x20" (180x50 cm).

Materials

Yarn: 2 skeins of Merino Lace by The Uncommon Thread (100% merino - 656 yd [600 m] - 100 g). Approx. 1200 yd [1097 m] of lace or light fingering weight yarn. The sample was made using colorway Birthstone.

Needles: US 5 (3.75 mm) needles.

Other: Stitch markers, row counter (optional), tapestry needle, crochet hook, waste yarn.

Gauge

22 stitches and 34 rows = 4" (10 cm) in Stockinette stitch on US 5 (3.75 mm) needles.

Finished Measurements

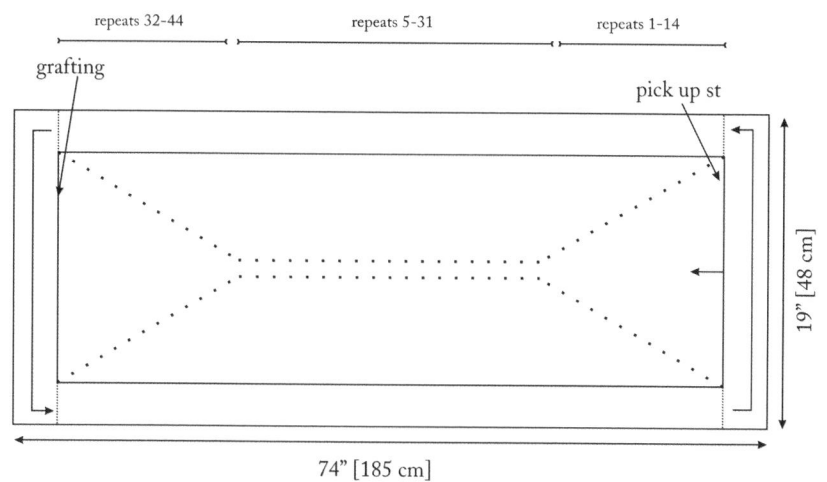

falling
Edge Piece

Provisionally CO 17 st.

Set-up Row: P to end.

Section 1 (corner)

Row 1: K1, p1, k11, W&T.
Row 2 (WS): P to 2 st from end, k1, p1.
Row 3: K1, p1, k to 1 st before last wrap, W&T.
Row 4: P to 2 st from end, k1, p1.

Repeat *rows 3 and 4* nine more times.

Next row (RS): K1, p1, W&T.
Next row (WS): K1, p1.
Row 25 (RS): K1, p1, k12, picking up wraps as you find them, and knitting them together with their corresponding st; pm, yo, k2tog, k1.
Row 26 (WS): Sl1, k1, p1, sm, p to 2 st from end, k1, p1.
Row 27: K1, p1, W&T.
Row 28: K1, p1.
Row 29: K1, p1, k1 together with wrap, W&T.
Row 30: P to 2 st from end, k1, p1.
Row 31: K1, p1, k to last wrap and knit it with its corresponding st, W&T.
Row 32: Same as row 30.

Repeat *rows 31 and 32* nine more times.

Row 51 (RS): K1, p1, k to last wrap and knit it with its corresponding st, sm, yo, k2tog, k1.
Row 52: Sl1, k1, p1, sm, p to 2 st from end, k1, p1.

Section 2

Row 1 (RS): K1, p1, k to 1 st before m, W&T.
Rows 2, 4 and 6: P to 2 st from end, k1, p1.
Rows 3 and 5: K1, p1, k to 2 st before last wrap, W&T.
Row 7 (RS): K1, p1, k to m, picking up wraps as you find them, and knitting them together with their corresponding st, sm, yo, k2tog, k1.
Row 8: Sl1, k1, p1, sm, p to 2 st from end, k1, p1.
Row 9: K1, p1, k to m, sm, yo, k2tog, k1.
Row 10: Same as row 8.

Repeat *rows 9 and 10* - four more times.

Work the whole Section 2 seven more times and then *rows 1-8* once more.

Section 3

Work as for Section 1 (on *row 25*, instead of pm, sm).

Next row (RS): K1, p1, k to m, sm, yo, k2tog, k1, pick up and knit 64 st along the edge of your piece.

Note: The pick-up ratio you should use is approx. 2 st for every 3 rows. It is tricky because the edge is worked in garter stitch, so what I do is: Pick up 1 st from in-between purl bumps, pick up 1 from the purl bump, pick up 1 from the next purl bump and pick up 1 from in-between. (You have just picked up 4 st out of 6 rows).

Unravel the provisionally CO st and place them on your left needle, ready to work a RS row: K1, ssk, yo, pm, k to 2 st from end, p1, k1.

Next row (WS): P1, k1, p to m, sm, p1, k2, pm, p64, pm, k2, p1, sm, p to 2 st from end, k1, p1. You should have 98 st.

Break yarn and put this piece on hold.

Work the whole *edge piece* once more, but don't put this one on hold. Continue working the following section.

Body of the shawl

First Repeat

Row 1 (RS): K1, p1, k to 1 st before m, W&T.

Rows 2, 4 and 6: P to 2 st from end, k1, p1.

Rows 3 and 5: K1, p1, k to 2 st before last wrap, W&T.

Row 7 (RS): K1, p1, k to m, picking up wraps as you find them, sm, yo, k2tog, k1, sm, k to next m, sm, k1, ssk, yo, sm, k to 2 st from end, p1, k1.

Row 8: P1, k1, p to 1 st before m, W&T.

Rows 9, 11 and 13: K to 2 st from end, p1, k1.

Rows 10 and 12: P1, k1, p to 2 st before last wrap, W&T.

Row 14 (WS): P1, k1, p to m, picking up wraps as you find them, and purling them together with their corresponding st, sm, p1, k2, sm, p to next m, sm, k2, p1, sm, p to 2 st from end, k1, p1.

Row 15: K1, p1, k to m, sm, yo, k2tog, k1, sm, k to next m, sm, k1, ssk, yo, sm, k to 2 st from end, p1, k1.

Row 16: P1, k1, p to m, sm, p1, k2, sm, p to next m, sm, k2, p1, sm, p to 2 st from end, k1, p1.

Repeat *rows 15-16* three more times.

Row 23: K1, p1, k to m, sm, yo, k2tog, k1, sm, k1, pm, k2tog, double yarn over, ssk, k to 5 st from next m, pm, k2tog, double yarn over, ssk, k1, sm, k1, ssk, yo, sm, k to 2 st from end, p1, k1.

Row 24: P1, k1, p to m, sm, p1, k2, sm, p3, k1, p1, sm, p to 4 st from next m, p2, k1, p1, sm, p to next m, sm, k2, p1, sm, p to 2 st from end, k1, p1.

Repeats 2-14

Row 1 (RS): K1, p1, k to 1 st before m, W&T.

Rows 2, 4 and 6: P to 2 st from end, k1, p1.

Rows 3 and 5: K1, p1, k to 2 st before last wrap, W&T.

Row 7 (RS): K1, p1, k to m, picking up wraps as you find them, and knitting them together with their corresponding st, sm, yo, k2tog, k1, sm, k to 3rd foll m, sm, k1, ssk, yo, sm, k to 2 st from end, p1, k1.

Row 8: P1, k1, p to 1 st before m, W&T.

Rows 9, 11 and 13: K to 2 st from end, p1, k1.

Rows 10 and 12: P1, k1, p to 2 st before last wrap, W&T.

Row 14 (WS): P1, k1, p to m, picking up wraps as you find them, and purling them together with their corresponding st, sm, p1, k2, sm, p to 3rd foll m, sm, k2, p1, sm, p to 2 st from end, k1, p1.

Row 15: K1, p1, k to m, sm, yo, k2tog, k1, sm, k to 3rd foll m, sm, k1, ssk, yo, sm, k to 2 st from end, p1, k1.

Row 16: P1, k1, p to m, sm, p1, k2, sm, p to 3rd foll m, sm, k2, p1, sm, p to 2 st from end, k1, p1.

Repeat *rows 15-16* three more times.

Row 23: K1, p1, k to m, sm, yo, k2tog, k1, sm, k to m, remove m, k2, pm, k2tog, double yarn over, ssk, k to 2 st before next m, slip 2 st from the LN to the RN, remove m, slip st back to LN, pm, k2tog, double yarn over, ssk, k to m, sm, k1, ssk, yo, sm, k to 2 st from end, p1, k1.

Row 24: P1, k1, p to m, sm, p1, k2, sm, p to 4 st from next m, p2, k1, p1, sm, p to 4 st from next m, p2, k1, p1, p to next m, sm, k2, p1, sm, p to 2 st from end, k1, p1.

Repeats 15-31

Work *rows 1-22* as for repeats 2-14.

Row 23: K1, p1, k to m, sm, yo, k2tog, k1, sm, k to m, sm, k2tog, double yarn over, ssk, k to m, sm, k2tog, double yarn over, ssk, k to m, sm, k1, ssk, yo, sm, k to 2 st from end, p1, k1.

Row 24: P1, k1, p to m, sm, p1, k2, sm, p to 4 st from next m, p2, k1, p1, sm, p to 4 st from next m, p2, k1, p1, p to next m, sm, k2, p1, sm, p to 2 st from end, k1, p1.

Repeats 32-44

Work *rows 1-22* as for repeats 2-14.

Row 23: K1, p1, k to m, sm, yo, k2tog, k1, sm, k to 2 st before m, slip 2 st from the LN to the RN, remove m, slip st back to the LN, pm, k2tog, double yarn over, ssk, k to m, remove m, k2, pm, k2tog, double yarn over, ssk, k to m, sm, k1, ssk, yo, sm, k to 2 st from end, p1, k1.

Row 24: P1, k1, p to m, sm, p1, k2, sm, p to 4 st from next m, p2, k1, p1, sm, p to 4 st from next m, p2, k1, p1, p to next m, sm, k2, p1, sm, p to 2 st from end, k1, p1.

After you finish your 44th repeat, work rows 1-22 once more.

Finishing

Place the *edge piece* you had on hold on a needle, and using tapestry needle, graft the end of your shawl to this piece.

Weave in ends, and block shawl to measurements, stretching out the fabric to achieve an open gauge.

salt and sand

by veera välimäki

This stylish little top is perfect for warm Spring and Summer days. The Salt and Sand top is finalized with elegant frills for the front and slight slits for both sides of the hem and back of the neck. It's easily worked from bottom up.

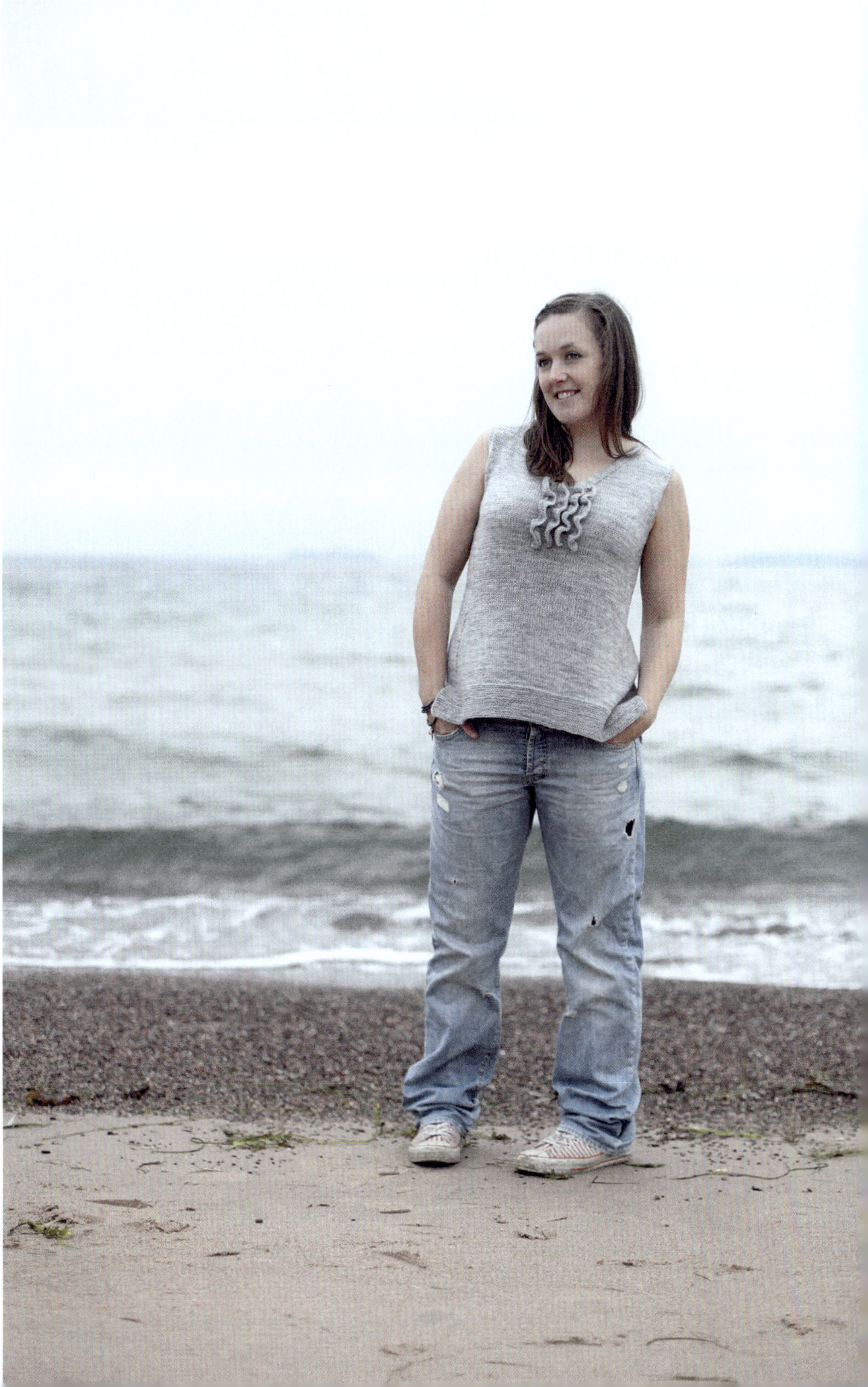

salt and sand

Sizes

XS (S, M, L, XL, XXL), shown in size S.
Finished chest circumference: 30 (34, 38, 42, 46, 50)" [75 (85, 95, 105, 115, 125) cm]. Choose a size with a small amount of positive ease.

Materials

Yarn: 2 (2, 3, 3, 3, 3) skeins of La Jolla by Baah! (100% Merino; 400 yd [366 m] - 100 g). Approx. 660 (745, 830, 930, 1050, 1150) yd [600 (680, 760, 850, 960, 1050) m] of fingering weight yarn. The sample was knit in colorway Grey Onyx.

Needles: US 4 [3.5 mm] circular needle, 32" [80 cm] long, and dpns. Adjust needle size if necessary to obtain the correct gauge.

Other: One ¾" [2 cm] button, stitch markers, pins, tapestry needle and blocking aids.

Gauge

23 stitches and 32 rows = 4" [10 cm] in Stockinette stitch.

Finished Measurements

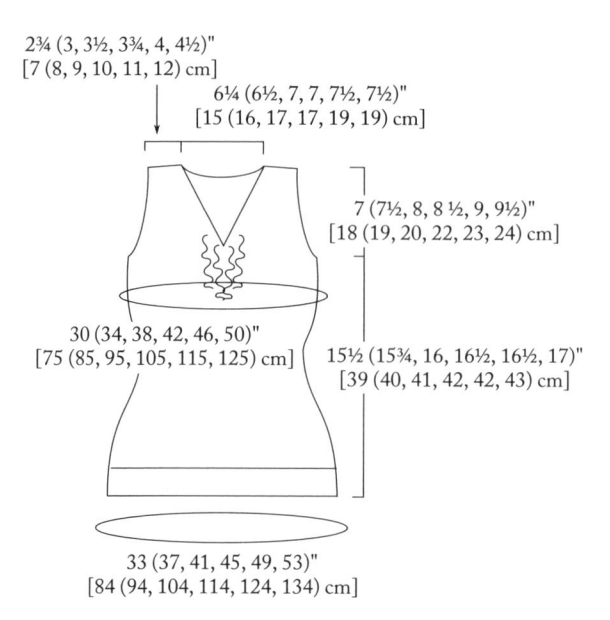

2¾ (3, 3½, 3¾, 4, 4½)"
[7 (8, 9, 10, 11, 12) cm]

6¼ (6½, 7, 7, 7½, 7½)"
[15 (16, 17, 17, 19, 19) cm]

7 (7½, 8, 8½, 9, 9½)"
[18 (19, 20, 22, 23, 24) cm]

30 (34, 38, 42, 46, 50)"
[75 (85, 95, 105, 115, 125) cm]

15½ (15¾, 16, 16½, 16½, 17)"
[39 (40, 41, 42, 42, 43) cm]

33 (37, 41, 45, 49, 53)"
[84 (94, 104, 114, 124, 134) cm]

salt and sand

Hem

Note: the top is worked from bottom up, joined in round after the garter stitch hem.

Back
Using circular needle, CO 96 (108, 120, 132, 142, 154). Do not join. Work back and forth in garter st (knit on RS and WS). Continue until the piece measures 2¾" [7 cm], ending with a WS row. Leave stitches on needle and cut yarn.

Front
CO another set of 96 (108, 120, 132, 142, 154) sts on same circ needle. Do not join. Work back and forth in garter st (knit on RS and WS). Continue until the piece measures 2¾" [7 cm], ending with a WS row. Leave stitches on needle and don't cut the yarn.

Body

Continue in Stockinette stitch, beginning with the front piece (RS) and join on first round as follows: Pm for beginning of round, knit all stitches of front, pm (for side), knit all stitches of back *[192 (216, 240, 264, 284, 308) sts on needle]*. Work 1¼" [3 cm] in St st and then begin waist shaping.

Decrease round (RS): *Sm, knit 9, ssk, knit until 11 sts before marker remain, k2tog, knit to marker; repeat once from *.

Repeat the *decrease round* every 4th round 7 more times *[32 sts decreased; 160 (184, 208, 232, 252, 276) sts on needle]*. Work 2" [5 cm] in Stockinette stitch. Begin waist increases.

Increase round (RS): *Sm, knit 10, m1L, knit until 10 sts before marker remain, m1R, knit to marker; repeat once from *.

Repeat the *increase round* every 4th round 2 more times *[12 sts increased; 172 (196, 220, 244, 264, 288) sts on needle]*. Work in Stockinette stitch, without increases, until the body measures 15½ (15¾, 16, 16½, 16½, 17)" [39 (40, 41, 42, 42, 43) cm] from cast-on edge.

Divide for front and back

BO for underarms on the dividing round

Next round (RS): *Remove marker, BO the first 4 (7, 10, 14, 15, 19) sts, knit until 4 (7, 10, 14, 15, 19) sts before marker remain, BO sts before marker; repeat from * once.

Cut yarn *[156 (168, 180, 188, 204, 212) sts remain; 78 (84, 90, 94, 102, 106) sts for each front and back]*.

Front

Attach yarn to the front stitches, the first half of stitches; 78 (84, 90, 94, 102, 106) stitches between the BO sts.

Side decrease row (RS): K1, p1, k1, p1, k2, ssk, knit until 8 sts remain, k2tog, k2, p1, k1, p1, k1.

Repeat the *side decrease row* on every RS row 4 more times and work all the WS rows in St st, but work the first/last sts in ribbing: (WS): p1, k1, p1, k1, purl until 4 sts remain, k1, p1, k1, p1. *After all decreases 68 (74, 80, 84, 92, 96) sts remain.*

Continue in Stockinette stitch and work the first and last 4 sts in 1X1 ribbing as established and add ribbing to the center for collar shaping

Center ribbing row (RS): K1, p1, k1, p1, knit 26 (29, 32, 34, 38, 40), p1 k1, p1, k2, p1, k1, p1, knit 26 (29, 32, 34, 38, 40) until 4 sts remain, p1, k1, p1, k1.

Center ribbing row (WS): Knit the knit sts and purl the purl sts.

Repeat the *center ribbing rows* once more.

Left front
Continue with first half of stitches, 34 (37, 40, 42, 46, 48) sts, only. Begin collar decreases on first row:

Decrease row (RS): K1, p1, k1, p1, knit until 8 sts remain, k2tog, k2, p1, k1, p1, k1.

Repeat the *decrease row* on every RS row 17 (18, 19, 19, 21, 21) more times [*16 (18, 20, 22, 24, 26) sts remain for shoulder*]. Continue without further decreases working in St st and keeping the last and first stitches in ribbing (knit the knits and purl the purls), until the armhole depth is 7 (7½, 8, 8 ½, 9, 9½)" [18 (19, 20, 22, 23, 24) cm]. Place sts on holder and cut yarn.

Right front

Join yarn to the RS of the 34 (37, 40, 42, 46, 48) stitches of right front. Begin collar decreases on first row:

Decrease row (RS): K1, p1, k1, p1, k2, ssk, knit until 4 sts remain, p1, k1, p1, k1.

Repeat the *decrease row* on every RS row 17 (18, 19, 19, 21, 21) more times [*16 (18, 20, 22, 24, 26) sts remain for shoulder*]. Continue without further decreases working in St st and keeping the last and first stitches in ribbing (knit the knits and purl the purls), until the armhole depth is 7 (7½, 8, 8 ½, 9, 9½)" [18 (19, 20, 22, 23, 24) cm]. Place sts on holder and cut yarn.

Back

Continue with the 78 (84, 90, 94, 102, 106) stitches of the back.

Side decrease row (RS): K1, p1, k1, p1, k2, ssk, knit until 8 sts remain, k2tog, k2, p1, k1, p1, k1.

Repeat the *side decrease row* on every RS row 4 more times and work all the WS rows in St st, but work the first/last 4 sts in ribbing [*(WS): p1, k1, p1, k1, purl until 4 sts remain, k1, p1, k1, p1*].

After all decreases 68 (74, 80, 84, 92, 96) sts remain. Continue in Stockinette stitch and work the first and last 4 sts in 1X1 ribbing as established until the armhole depth is 3 (3½, 4, 4½, 5, 5½)" [8 (9, 10, 12, 13, 14) cm].

Add ribbing to the center for collar shaping:

Center ribbing row (RS): K1, p1, k1, p1, knit 26 (29, 32, 34, 38, 40), p1 k1, p1, k2, p1, k1, p1, knit 26 (29, 32, 34, 38, 40) until 4 sts remain, p1, k1, p1, k1.

Center ribbing row (WS): Knit the knit sts and purl the purl sts.

Repeat the *center ribbing rows* once more.

Right back

Continue with first half of stitches, 34 (37, 40, 42, 46, 48) sts, only.

Row 1 (RS): K1, p1, k1, p1, knit until 4 sts remain, p1, k1, p1, k1.

Row 2 (WS): P1, k1, p1, k1, p until 4 sts remain, k1, p1, k1, p1.

Work *rows 1 and 2* until the armhole depth is 5 (5½, 6, 6 ½, 7, 7½)" [13 (14, 15, 17, 18, 19) cm]. Add back of the neck ribbing:

Row 3 (RS): K1, p1, k1, p1, knit 12 (13, 16, 18, 20, 22), *p1, k1; repeat from * to end.

Row 4 (WS): Knit the knit sts and purl the purl sts.

Work *rows 3 and 4* once more. Work buttonhole on next row (RS): K1, p1, k1, p1, knit 12 (13, 16, 18, 20, 22), *p1, k1; repeat from * until 4 sts remain, yo, k2tog, p1, k1. Work rows 4, 3 and 4 once more. BO neck sts and begin neck shaping on next row: K1, p1, k1, p1, knit 8 (9, 12, 14, 16, 18), k2tog, k2, p1, k1, p1, k1, BO the remaining sts in ribbing. Cut yarn.

Join yarn to the remaining 19 (20, 23, 25, 27, 29) stitches of right back, WS facing. Continue to work the first and last 4 sts in ribbing (knit the knits and purl the purls) and continue neck shaping on every RS row for 3 (2, 3, 3, 3, 3) times: K1, p1, k1, p1, knit until 8 sts remain, k2tog, k2, p1, k1, p1, k1. After all decreases continue without shaping until the armhole depth is 7 (7½, 8, 8 ½, 9, 9½)" [18 (19, 20, 22, 23, 24) cm].

Join Right Shoulder

Place right front stitches on one dpn and turn garment WS facing. Hold both shoulder stitch sets parallel and BO shoulder sts using three-needle BO. *Note: you can also graft the shoulder stitches.*

Left back

Continue with the remaining half of back stitches, 34 (37, 40, 42, 46, 48) sts.

Row 1 (RS): K1, p1, k1, p1, knit until 4 sts remain, p1, k1, p1, k1.

Row 2 (WS): P1, k1, p1, k1, p until 4 sts remain, k1, p1, k1, p1.

Work *rows 1 and 2* until the armhole depth is 5 (5½, 6, 6 ½, 7, 7½)" [13 (14, 15, 17, 18, 19) cm].

Add back of the neck ribbing:

> *Row 3 (RS):* *k1, p1; repeat from * until 16 (17, 20, 22, 24, 26) sts remain, knit 12 (13, 16, 18, 20, 22), p1, k1, p1, k1.
>
> *Row 4 (WS):* Knit the knit sts and purl the purl sts.

Work *rows 3 and 4* three times more. BO neck sts and begin neck shaping on next row: BO sts in ribbing, until 20 (21, 24, 26, 28, 30) stitches remain, k1, p1, k1, p1, k2, ssk, knit until 4 sts remain, p1, k1, p1, k1.

Continue with the remaining 19 (20, 23, 25, 27, 29) stitches of right back, with a WS. Work as established in St st and the first and last 4 sts in ribbing (knit the knits and purl the purls). Continue neck shaping on every RS row for 3 (2, 3, 3, 3, 3) times: K1, p1, k1, p1, k2, ssk, knit until 4 sts remain, p1, k1, p1, k1. After all decreases continue without shaping until the armhole depth is 7 (7½, 8, 8 ½, 9, 9½)" [18 (19, 20, 22, 23, 24) cm].

> **Join Left Shoulder**
>
> Place left front stitches on one dpn and turn garment WS facing. Hold both shoulder stitch sets parallel and BO shoulder sts using three-needle BO. *Note: you can also graft the shoulder stitches.*

Frills

Note: the placement of frills can be easily modified. Mark with pins the correct measurements of the frills before picking up stitches. The two center frills are shorter than the frills on sides. You should have approx. ¾" [2 cm] vertical spaces between each frill. You can also work the frills using circular needle.

First frill (longer frill on right side)

Mark the beginning spot of the frill: 5" [13 cm] straight down from the beginning of the collar shaping. Using one dpn, pick up and knit 28 sts straight up to the beginning of collar shaping (up to the first decreased stitch, that's the end of the frill).

Work back and forth in garter stitch and increase on next row: k1fb all sts [*56 sts on needle*].

Shape the frill with short rows

> *Next two rows:* knit until 1 sts remains, W&T.

> *Next 4 rows:* knit until 1 st before previous wrapped st remains, W&T.

Knit to end on next row (no need to pick up wraps, they will blend in garter st) and BO all frill sts on next row.

Second frill (shorter frill on right side)

Mark the beginning spot of the frill: 4" [10 cm] straight down from the middle, from second knit stitch on right side of the collar ribbing. Using one dpn, pick up and knit 24 sts straight up to second knit stitch of the collar ribbing.

Work back and forth in garter stitch and increase on next row: k1fb all sts [*48 sts on needle*]. Work the short rows and BO as on the first frill.

Third frill (shorter frill on left side)

Mark the beginning spot of the frill: 4" [10 cm] straight down from the second knit stitch on left side of the collar ribbing. Using one dpn, pick up and knit 24 sts straight up to second knit stitch of the collar ribbing.

Work back and forth in garter stitch and increase on next row: k1fb all sts [*48 sts on needle*]. Work the short rows and BO as on the first frill.

Fourth frill (longer frill on left side)

Mark the beginning spot of the frill: 5" [13 cm] straight down from the beginning of the collar shaping. Using one dpn, pick up and knit 28 sts straight up to the beginning of collar shaping (up to the first decreased stitch, that's the end of the frill).

Work back and forth in garter stitch and increase on next row: k1fb all sts [*56 sts on needle*]. Work the short rows and BO as on the first frill.

Finishing

Weave in all yarn ends, sew on button to the back and block the sweater using your preferred method.

unimaginable

Will you dare to walk beyond the woods towards the unknown?

Sometimes as designers we feel this way. We have an idea of a shape, a contrast or a movement and we can't really get it out of our heads until we fully explore it and unravel its mysteries as elements of a magical forest.

The process of unfolding an idea into a design without knowing how to achieve it, but knowing what it will become is what moves us to try something new and inspiring.

With these designs, we invite you to take a trip to a fairytale land and think of your knitting as stories that will have a beginning and an unimaginable ending. Might even be something out of this world!

41

unimaginable

fly forward shawl

adventurous cardigan

adventurous

by joji locatelli

When you learned to knit, you probably were afraid of making mistakes and felt intimidated by any new technique. There was just so much to learn! But as you completed projects, you learned that knitting is an adventure enriched by experiences, and there's always a chance to learn something from anything you make.

You are now confident enough with your knitting techniques and you want to take a step forward and make something striking! Let your stitches glow with the beautiful cables in this masterpiece coat. Make your knitting an exciting adventure every time!

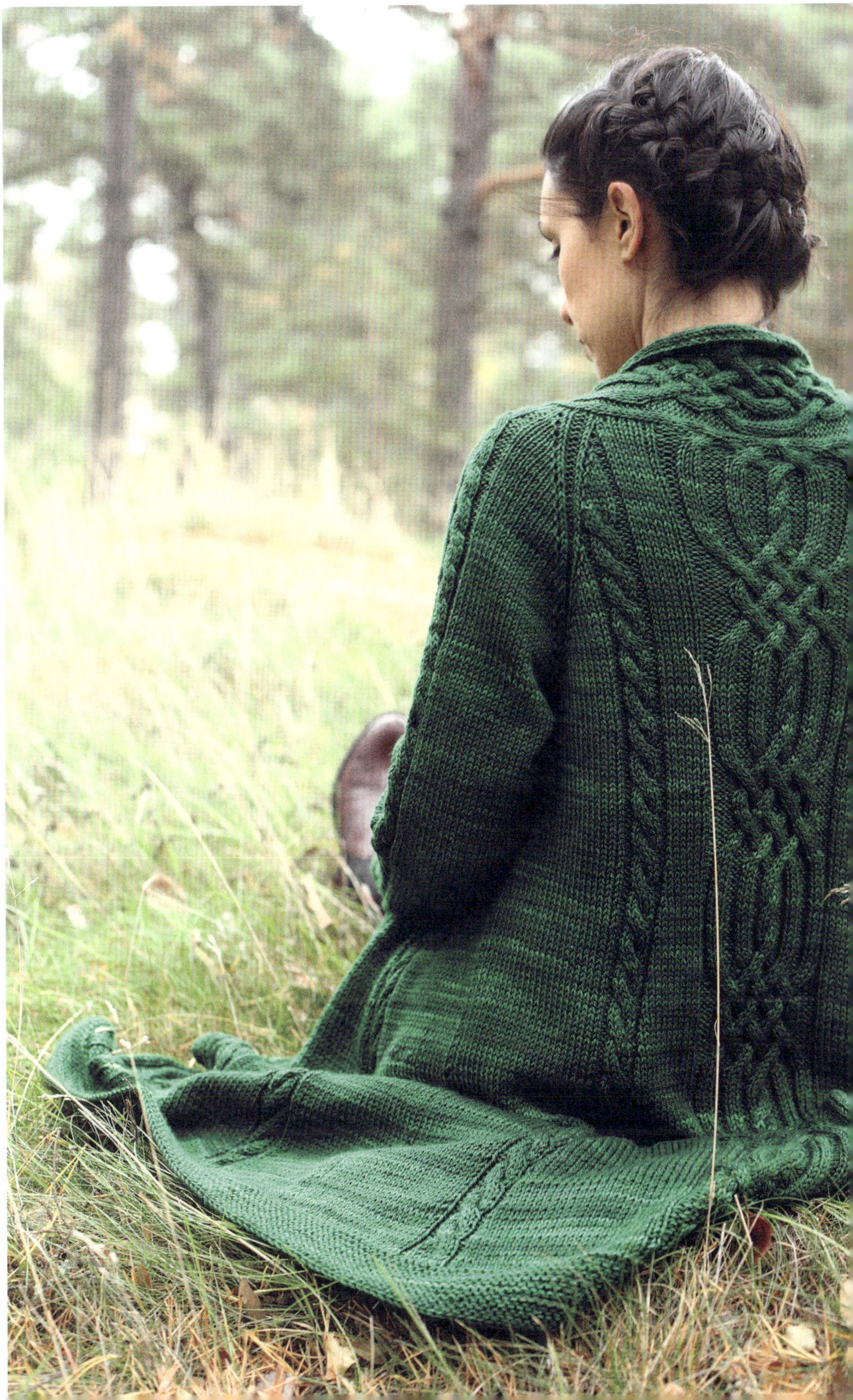

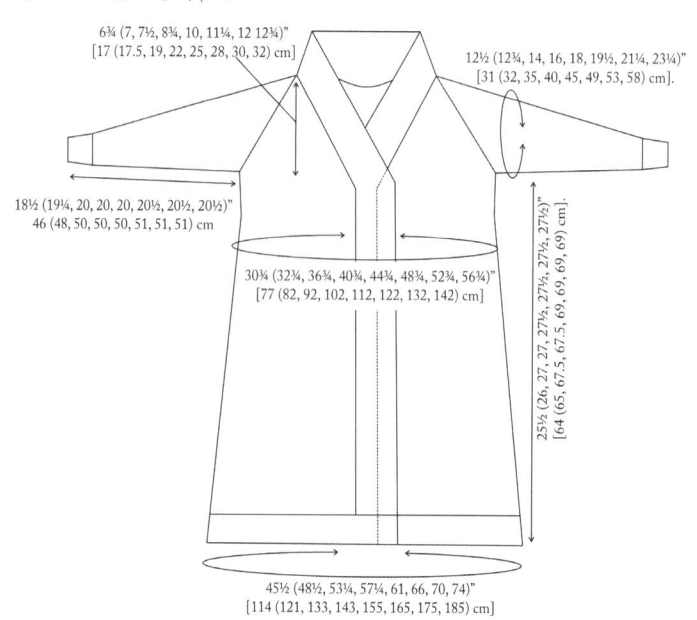

adventurous

Sizes

XS (S, M, L, XL, XXL, 3XL, 4XL). Shown in size M.

Finished bust circumference (Worn closed, with collar bands overlapped): 30¾ (32¾, 36¾, 40¾, 44¾, 48¾, 52¾, 56¾)" [77 (82, 92, 102, 112, 122, 132, 142) cm]. *Note: See more detailed finished measurements below in schematics picture or written on page 51.*

Materials

Yarn: 7 (7, 8, 8, 9, 9, 10, 10) skeins of Superwash DK by SweetGeorgia Yarns (100% merino; 265 yd [242 m] - 115 g). Approx. 1700 (1850, 1980, 2100, 2250, 2350, 2500, 2600) yd [1554 (1692, 1811, 1920, 2057, 2148, 2286, 2377) m] of DK weight yarn. The sample was knit in size M using the colorway English Ivy.

Needles: US 6 [4 mm] and US 4 [3.5 mm] circular needles.

Other: Crochet hook for provisional CO, cable needle, st markers in 3 different colors (if you don't have different color stitch markers, you can just use little loops of yarn), waste yarn or stitch holders.

Gauge

Stockinette stitch: 20 st and 27 rows = 4" (10 cm) after blocking.
Cabled pattern: 38 st and 27 rows = 4" (10 cm) after blocking.

Finished Measurements

6¾ (7, 7½, 8¾, 10, 11¼, 12 12¾)"
[17 (17.5, 19, 22, 25, 28, 30, 32) cm]

12½ (12¾, 14, 16, 18, 19½, 21¼, 23¼)"
[31 (32, 35, 40, 45, 49, 53, 58) cm].

18½ (19¼, 20, 20, 20, 20½, 20½, 20½)"
46 (48, 50, 50, 50, 51, 51, 51) cm

30¾ (32¾, 36¾, 40¾, 44¾, 48¾, 52¾, 56¾)"
[77 (82, 92, 102, 112, 122, 132, 142) cm]

25½ (26, 27, 27, 27½, 27½, 27½, 27½)"
[64 (65, 67.5, 67.5, 69, 69, 69, 69) cm].

45½ (48½, 53¼, 57¼, 61, 66, 70, 74)"
[114 (121, 133, 143, 155, 165, 175, 185) cm]

adventurous

Stitches used

Cable A (worked over 38 st)
   See chart on page 51.

Cable B Left (worked over 10 st)
   Row 1: P2, C6F (slip 3 st onto cable needle, hold in front, k3, k3 from CN), p2.
   Rows 2, 4, 6: K2, p6, k2.
   Rows 3, 5: P2, k6, p2.

Cable B Right (worked over 10 st)
   Row 1: P2, C6B (slip 3 st onto cable needle, hold in back, k3, k3 from CN), p2.
   Rows 2, 4, 6: K2, p6, k2.
   Rows 3, 5: P2, k6, p2.

Right Back Collar

With US6 (4 mm) needles, provisionally CO 44 st.
   Set-up row (WS): P3, k2, p3, k4, p3, k4, p6, k4, p3, k4, p3, k2, p3.
   Next row (RS): K3, work Row 1 of Cable A (see Chart at the end of the pattern), k3.
   Next row (WS): P3, work foll row of Cable A, p3.

Continue working in the established pattern (3 Stockinette st at each edge and always working the foll row of the cable) until your piece measures approx. 9" (23 cm), ending with a WS row (take note of the last row of the chart you worked, so you can work the other half of the collar to the same row). Break yarn and put all st on hold.

left Back Collar

Unravel the provisionally CO st and work exactly as you did for the Right Back collar, starting with the Set-up row. Place a safety pin or a split-ring st marker to indicate where you re-joined your yarn. This will indicate the middle point of your collar.

Do not break yarn after working the last WS row.

Yoke

   Row 1 (RS): K3, work foll row of Cable A, k3. Now start picking up stitches along the edge of your Collar. Pick up 43 st at each side of the split ring marker that indicates the "middle" point of your collar. Now place the held stitches from the Right collar onto the needles. K3, work foll row of Cable A, k3.

Note: On the following row you place your markers. There will be neckline markers (Nm), raglan markers (Rm) and cable markers (Cm). I suggest you use different colors for each (if you have them), or at least for the cable markers, since you won't be working any increases/decreases near those.

   Row 2 (WS): P3, work foll row of Cable A, p3, place "neckline marker" (pNm), p2, k1, place

47

raglan marker (pRm), k1, p1, k2, p6, k2, p1, k1, pRm, k1, p6, place cable marker (pCm), work Cable A, starting on the same row you just worked for the collar, pCm, p6, k1, pRm, k1, p1, k2, p6, k2, p1, k1, pRm, k1, p2, pNm, p3, work foll row of Cable A, p3.

You should have a total of 174 st: 44 for each collar band, 3 for each front, 14 for each sleeve and 52 for the back.

Row 3: Work in patt to m, sm, k1, m1L, k1, p1, sm, p1, k1, m1R, p2, k6, p2, m1L, k1, p1, sm, p1, k1, m1R, k to m, sm, work Cable A, sm, k to 2 st before m, m1L, k1, p1, sm, p1, k1, m1R, p2, k6, p2, m1L, k1, p1, sm, p1, k1, m1R, k1, sm, work in patt to end. *8 st increased.*

You should have a total of 182 st: 44 for each collar band, 4 for each front, 16 for each sleeve and 54 for the back.

Row 4 and all foll WS rows: Work all st as they appear (knit the knit st and purl the purl st).

Row 5: Work in patt to m, sm, k2, m1Lp, k1, p1, sm, p1, k1, m1R, k1, pCm, work row 1 of Cable B LEFT (worked over 10 st), pCm, k to 2 st before m, m1L, k1, p1, sm, p1, k1, m1Rp, k to m, sm, work Cable A, sm, k to 2 st before m, m1Lp, k1, p1, sm, p1, k1, m1R, k1, pCm, work row 1 of Cable B RIGHT, pCm, k to 2 st before m, m1L, k1, p1, sm, p1, k1, m1Rp, k to m, sm, work in patt to end. *8 st increased.*

Row 7: Work in patt to m, sm, m1R, k2, pCm, p1, m1Lp, k1, p1, sm, *p1, k1, m1R, k to m, sm, Cable B LEFT, sm, k to 2 st before m, m1L, k1, p1* (from now on, the sentence between * will be written as "work left sleeve in patt"), sm, p1, k1, m1Rp, p1, pCm, k to m, sm, work Cable A, sm, k to 3 st before m, pCm, p1, m1Lp, k1, p1, sm, *p1, k1, m1R, k to m, sm, Cable B RIGHT, sm, k to 2 st before m, m1L, k1, p1*(from now on, the sentence between * will be written as "work right sleeve in patt"), sm, p1, k1, m1Rp, p1, pCm, k to m, sm, m1L, sm, work in patt to end. *10 st increased.*

You should have a total of 200 st: 44 for each collar band, 7 for each front, 20 for each sleeve and 58 for the back.

Left Sleeve in patt: P1, k1, m1R, k to m, sm, Cable B LEFT, sm, k to 2 st before m, m1L, k1, p1

Right Sleeve in patt: P1, k1, m1R, k to m, sm, Cable B RIGHT, sm, k to 2 st before m, m1L, k1, p1

Row 9: Work in patt to m, sm, k to m, sm, p2, m1L, k1, p1, sm, work left sleeve in patt, sm, p1, k1, m1R, p2, sm, k to m, sm, work Cable A, sm, k to m, sm, p2, m1L, k1, p1, sm, work right sleeve in patt, sm, p1, k1, m1R, p2, sm, k to m, sm, work in patt to end. *8 st increased.*

Row 11: Work in patt to m, sm, k to m, sm, p2, k1, m1L, k1, p1, sm, work left sleeve in patt, sm, p1, k1, m1R, k1, p2, sm, k to m, sm, work Cable A, sm, k to m, sm, p2, k1, m1L, k1, p1, sm, work right sleeve in patt, sm, p1, k1, m1R, k1, p2, sm, k to m, sm, work in patt to end. *8 st increased.*

Row 13: Work in patt to m, sm, m1R, k to m, sm, p2, k to 2 st before m, m1L, k1, p1, sm, work left sleeve in patt, sm, p1, k1, m1R, k to 2 st before m, p2, sm, k to m, sm, work Cable A, sm, k to m, sm, p2, k to 2 st before m, m1L, k1, p1, sm, work right sleeve in patt, sm, p1, k1, m1R, k to 2 st before m, p2, sm, k to m, m1L, sm, work in patt to end. *10 st increased.*

Row 15: Work in patt to m, sm, k to m, sm, p2, k to 2 st before m, m1L, k1, p1, sm, work left sleeve in patt, sm, p1, k1, m1R, k to 2 st before m, p2, sm, k to m, sm, work Cable A, sm, k to m, sm, p2, k to 2 st before m, m1L, k1, p1, sm, work right sleeve in patt, sm, p1, k1, m1R, k to 2 st before m, p2, sm, k to m, sm, work in patt to end. *8 st increased.*

Row 17: Same as 15. *8 st increased.*

Row 19: Same as 13. *10 st increased.*

Row 21: Work in patt to m, sm, k to m, sm, p2, k to 2 st before m, m1Lp, k1, p1, sm, work left sleeve in patt, sm, p1, k1, m1Rp, k to 2 st before m, p2, sm, k to m, sm, work Cable A, sm, k to m, sm, p2, k to 2 st before m, m1Lp, k1, p1, sm, work right sleeve in patt, sm, p1, k1, m1Rp, k to 2 st before m, p2, sm, k to m, sm, work in patt to end. *8 st increased.*

Row 23: Work in patt to m, sm, k to m, sm, p2, C6B, p1, m1Lp, k1, p1, sm, work left sleeve in patt, sm, p1, k1, m1Rp, p1, C6F, p2, sm, k to m, sm, work Cable A, sm, k to m, sm, p2, C6B, p1, m1Lp, k1, p1, sm, work right sleeve in patt, sm, p1, k1, m1Rp, p1, C6F, p2, sm, k to m, sm, work in patt to end. *8 st increased.*

Row 25: Work in patt to m, sm, m1R, k to m, sm, work Cable B RIGHT, pCm, m1L, k1, p1, sm, work left sleeve in patt, sm, p1, k1, m1R, pCm, work Cable B LEFT, sm, k to m, sm, work Cable A, sm, k to m, sm, work Cable B RIGHT, pCm, m1L, k1, p1, sm, work right sleeve in patt, sm, p1, k1, m1R, pCm, work Cable B LEFT, sm, k to m, m1L, sm, work in patt to end. *10 st increased.*

Row 27: Work in patt to m, sm, k to m, sm, Cable B RIGHT, sm, k to 2 st from m, m1L, k1, p1, sm, work left sleeve in patt, sm, p1, k1, m1R, k to m, sm, Cable B LEFT, sm, k to m, sm, work Cable A, sm, k to m, sm, Cable B RIGHT, sm, k to 2 st from m, m1L, k1, p1, sm, work right sleeve in patt, sm, p1, k1, m1R, k to m, sm, Cable B LEFT, sm, k to m, sm, work in patt to end. *8 st increased.*

You should have a total of 286 st: 44 for each collar band, 20 for each front, 40 for each sleeve and 78 for the back.

Work a WS row.

Repeat the last 2 rows 10 (11, 13, 17, 21, 25, 28, 31) more times. *You should have a total of 366 (374, 390, 422, 454, 486, 510, 534) st: 44 for each collar band, 30 (31, 33, 37, 41, 45, 48, 51) st for each front, 60 (62, 66, 74, 82, 90, 96, 102) for each sleeve and 98 (100, 104, 112, 120, 128, 134, 140) for the back.*

Divide for body and sleeves

Next row (RS): Work in pattern to 2 st before 1st raglan marker, m1L, k2, slip the foll 60 (62, 66, 74, 82, 90, 96, 102) stitches onto a piece of waste yarn (removing markers), put them on hold. CO 1 (2, 5, 6, 7, 8, 9, 11) st, pm, CO1, pm, CO 1 (2, 5, 6, 7, 8, 9, 11) st, k2, m1R, work in patt to 2 st before next raglan marker, m1L, k2, slip the foll 60 (62, 66, 74, 82, 90, 96, 102)

st onto a piece of waste yarn (removing markers), put them on hold, CO 1 (2, 5, 6, 7, 8, 9, 11) st, pm, CO1, pm, CO 1 (2, 5, 6, 7, 8, 9, 11) st, k2, m1R, work in patt to end of row.

You should now have 256 (264, 284, 304, 324, 344, 360, 380) st: 44 for each collar section, 32 (34, 39, 44, 49, 54, 58, 63) for each front, 1 "seam" st at each side and 102 (106, 116, 126, 136, 146, 154, 164) st for the back.

> *Next row (WS):* Work in patt to side marker, sm, k1, sm, work in patt to next side marker, sm, k1, sm, work in patt to end of row.

Continue working in pattern, always working the following rows of your cables and working the "seam" stitches in reverse Stockinette st until your work measures 3½" (9 cm) from your armhole, ending with a WS row.

> *Next row (RS):* Work collar st in pattern, sm, k to next marker (Cm), m1L, sm, work in patt to 3 st before side marker, k2tog, k1, sm, p1, sm, k1, ssk, k to next m, (Cm), sm, work in patt to next m (Cm), sm, m1R, k to next m, sm, work in patt to next m, sm, k to next m, m1L, sm, work in patt to 3 st before side marker, k2tog, k1, sm, p1, sm, k1, ssk, k to next m, sm, work in patt to next m, sm, m1R, work in patt to end of row.

Work 5 more rows in pattern, without any increases/decreases.

> *Next row (RS):* Work collar st in pattern, sm, k to next marker (Cm), m1L, sm, work in patt to side marker, sm, p1, sm, k to next m, (Cm), sm, work in patt to next m (Cm), sm, m1R, k to next m, sm, work in patt to next m, sm, k to next m, m1L, sm, work in patt to side marker, sm, p1, sm, k to next m, sm, work in patt to next m, sm, m1R, work in patt to end of row. *4 st increased.*

Work 5 rows in pattern, without any increases/decreases. Repeat the last 6 rounds and continue working in this manner until your garment measures 22½ (23, 24, 24, 24½, 24½, 24½, 24½)" [56.5 (57.5, 60, 60, 61.5, 61.5, 61.5, 61.5)] cm from your underarm, or 3" [7.5 cm] less than your desired length.

Hem

The hem is worked in garter st (knit all rows), so the specific st count is not important, but since the gauge in garter stitch is much looser than with the cables, several stitches need to be decreased. Switch to US 4 [3.5 mm] needles.

> *Next row (RS):* Knit the collar stitches decreasing 7 st in this section; remove m (rm), k to next m, rm, k2tog, k2, k2tog, k2, k2tog, rm, k to side m, rm, k1, rm, k to next m, rm, k2tog, k2, k2tog, k2, k2tog, rm, k to next m, knit all stitches of the central cable and decrease 7 st in this section, rm, k to next m, rm, k2tog, k2, k2tog, k2, k2tog, k to side m, rm, k1, rm, k to next m, k2tog, k2, k2tog, k2, k2tog, rm, k to next m, knit the collar stitches decreasing 7 st in this section.

Work 21 more rows in garter st, and on the following row bind off all st.

Sleeves

With US 6 (4 mm) needles, and starting at the center armhole, pick up and knit 3 (4, 5, 6, 7, 7, 8, 10) st (this number of stitches might be different than the st you CO for the underarm, so you might need to skip some spots while picking up stitches). Place the 60 (62, 66, 74, 82, 90, 96, 102) held stitches of a sleeve onto the left needle, work in patt to end of round. Pick up and knit 2 (3, 4, 5, 6, 6, 7, 9) more stitches, reaching the center of the armhole again. Place marker. *You should have 65 (69, 75, 85, 95, 103, 111, 121) st*

> *Next round:* P1 (this will be your "seam" st), work in patt to the end of round (knitting all the rest of the new stitches, and working the foll row of the corresponding cable)

Continue working in pattern until sleeve measures 4" (10 cm) from the point where you picked up your stitches.

> *Next round (decrease round):* P1, k2tog, work in patt to 2 st from end, ssk.

Continue working in pattern repeating a decrease round every 14 (12, 12, 7, 6, 5, 5, 4) rounds 5 (6, 6, 11, 12, 15, 17, 19) more times. *You should have 53 (55, 61, 61, 69, 71, 75, 81) st.*

When sleeve measures 15½ (16¼, 17, 17, 17, 17½, 17½, 17½)" [39.5 (40.5, 42.5, 42.5, 42.5, 43.5, 43.5, 43.5) cm] or 3" [7.5 cm] less than your desired length. Switch to smaller needles and start cuff.

> *Next round:* P1, *K5, k2tog* 7 (7, 8, 8, 9, 10,

10, 11) times, k to end.

Next round: P to end.

Next round: P1, k to end.

Repeat the last 2 rounds 15 more times. On the foll row BO all st.

Finishing

Weave in ends and block garment to finished measurements.

Finished Measurements

Bust circumference (Worn closed, with collar bands overlapped): 30¾ (32¾, 36¾, 40¾, 44¾, 48¾, 52¾, 56¾)" [77 (82, 92, 102, 112, 122, 132, 142) cm].

Bottom circumference: 45½ (48½, 53¼, 57¼, 61, 66, 70, 74)" [114 (121, 133, 143, 155, 165, 175, 185) cm].

Yoke depth: 6¾ (7, 7½, 8¾, 10, 11¼, 12 12¾)" [17 (17.5, 19, 22, 25, 28, 30, 32) cm].

Upper sleeve circumference: 12½ (12¾, 14, 16, 18, 19½, 21¼, 23¼)" [31 (32, 35, 40, 45, 49, 53, 58) cm].

Sleeve length from underarm to cuff: 18½ (19¼, 20, 20, 20, 20½, 20½, 20½)" [46 (48, 50, 50, 50, 51, 51, 51) cm].

Length from underarm to hem: 25½ (26, 27, 27, 27½, 27½, 27½, 27½)" [64 (65, 67.5, 67.5, 69, 69, 69, 69) cm].

Cable A

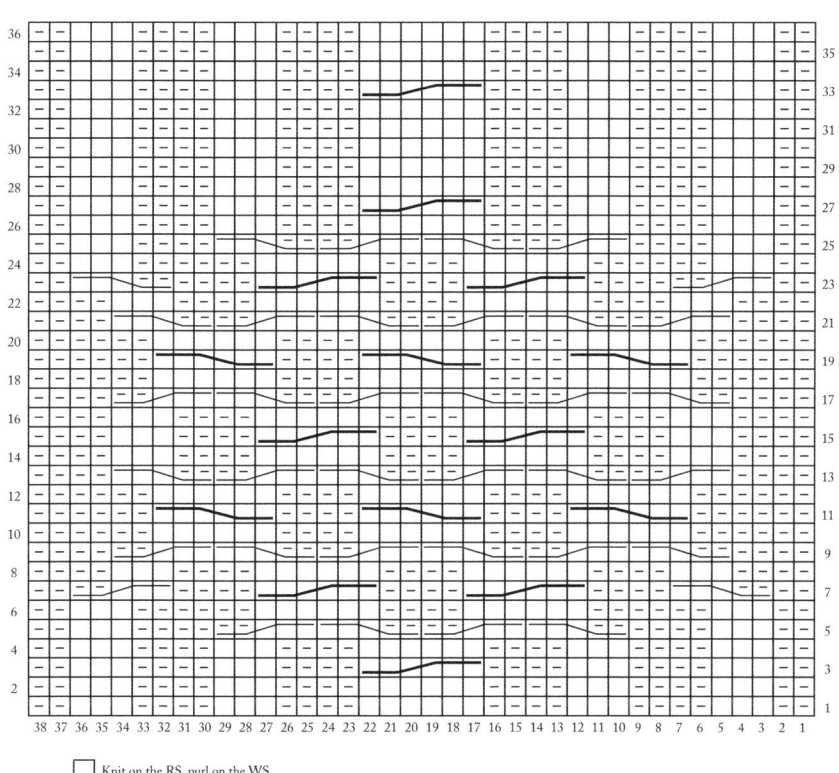

☐ Knit on the RS, purl on the WS

– Purl on the RS, knit on the WS

Slip 2 onto cable needle, hold in back, k3, p2 from CN.

Slip 3 onto cable needle, hold in front, p2, k3 from CN.

Slip 3 onto cable needle, hold in back, k3, k3 from CN.

Slip 3 onto cable needle, hold in front, k3, k3 from CN.

51

fly forward

by veera välimäki

Squishy merino wool is paired with simple ingredients: garter stitch and twisted ribbing with some short rows to keep the process smooth. The shawl has an almost unimaginable flow from the repeat of the two sections. Unimaginably easy and fun to knit as well and wonderfully warm to wrap around your neck.

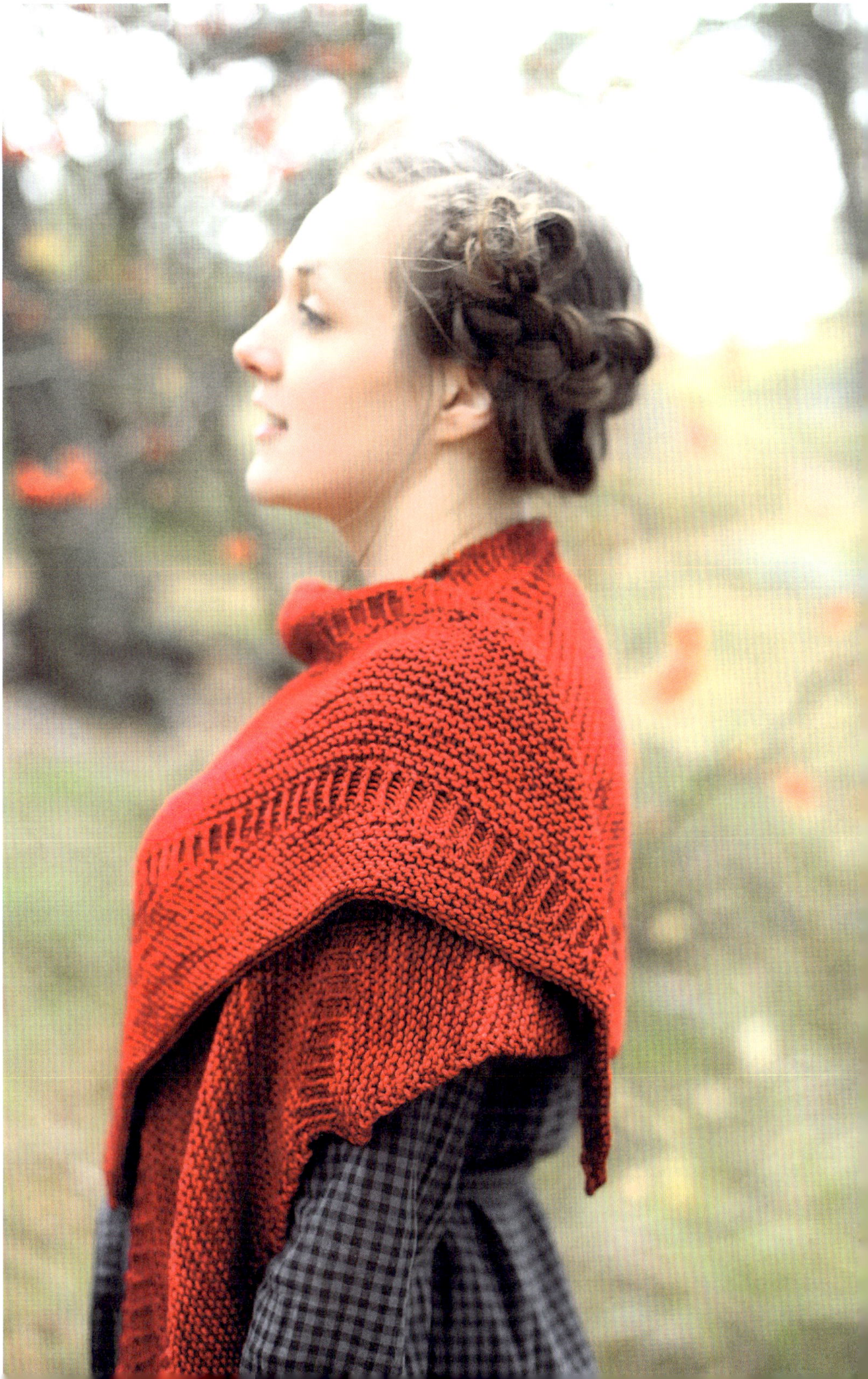

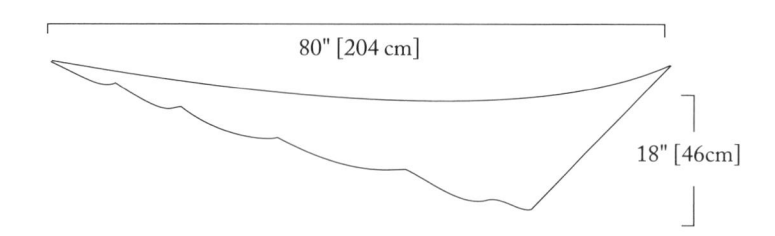

fly forward

Sizes

One size
Finished measurements: 18" [46 cm] deep and 80" [204 cm] long, after blocking.

Materials

Yarn: 3 skeins of Hayden DK by Lakes Yarn & Fiber (100% superwash merino; 280 yd [256 m] - 100 g). Approx. 690 yd [630 m] of heavy DK weight yarn. The sample was knit in colorway Letter A.

Needles: US 8 [5 mm] circular needle, 32" [80 cm] long or longer. Adjust needle size if necessary to obtain the correct gauge.

Other: Tapestry needle and blocking aids.

Gauge

18 stitches and 36 rows = 4" [10 cm] in garter stitch.

Finished Measurements

fly forward

Shawl

CO 3 stitches.

*

Garter stitch part

Row 1 (RS): Knit until 2 sts remain, k1fb, k1.
Row 2 (WS): K1fb, knit to end.
Row 3 (RS): Knit 1, k2tog, knit until 2 sts remain, k1fb, k1.
Row 4 (WS): K1fb, knit to end.

Work *rows 1–4* five more times.

Twisted ribbing

Continue in twisted ribbing (*k1tbl, p1tbl; repeat to end*).

Row 5 (RS): Work in twisted ribbing until 2 sts remain, k/p1fb (keep ribbing continuous), k1.
Row 6 (WS): K1fb, work to end in twisted ribbing.

Repeat *rows 5 and 6* twice more.

Short rows

Continue with short rows and work in garter stitch. *Note: There's no need to pick up the wraps, as they will blend in garter stitch nicely.*

Row 7 (RS): Knit 3, W&T.
Rows 8, 10 and 12 (WS): Knit to end.
Row 9 (RS): Knit 1, k2tog, knit 2 sts past the previous wrapped stitch, W&T.
Row 11 (WS): Knit 2 sts past the previous wrapped stitch, W&T.

Repeat *rows 9–12* until less than 5 stitches remain after wrapped stitch on RS.

*

Repeat these 3 sections: GARTER STITCH PART, TWISTED RIBBING and SHORT ROWS until you have 7 ribbings or until you run out of yarn. *Note: you don't need to complete all the short rows after the last ribbing, or you can add one more set of repeats if you have enough yarn.*

BO all stitches loosely on next RS row.

Finishing

Weave in ends and block shawl to finished measurements.

focus

There is a thing in this world I have yet to master, one that may take years, possibly a lifetime to get and that is focus. Why is it so difficult in this day and age to focus on something? The amount of distractions presented to us moment to moment is vast. We are literally inundated with stimuli.

There is always something that needs doing and there will always be someone waiting to hear from you. I say, put your phones down for a minute, lift your head up and look high. There is a world swirling around you and you might be missing it.

Focus on your today in the here and now and how you can make your next moments count. What is really going to make your life better? If you had only hours left what would you do with that time? Focus on getting balance back and whenever possible, simplify.

Do it today, there is no better time than now to focus on what you want and make it happen.

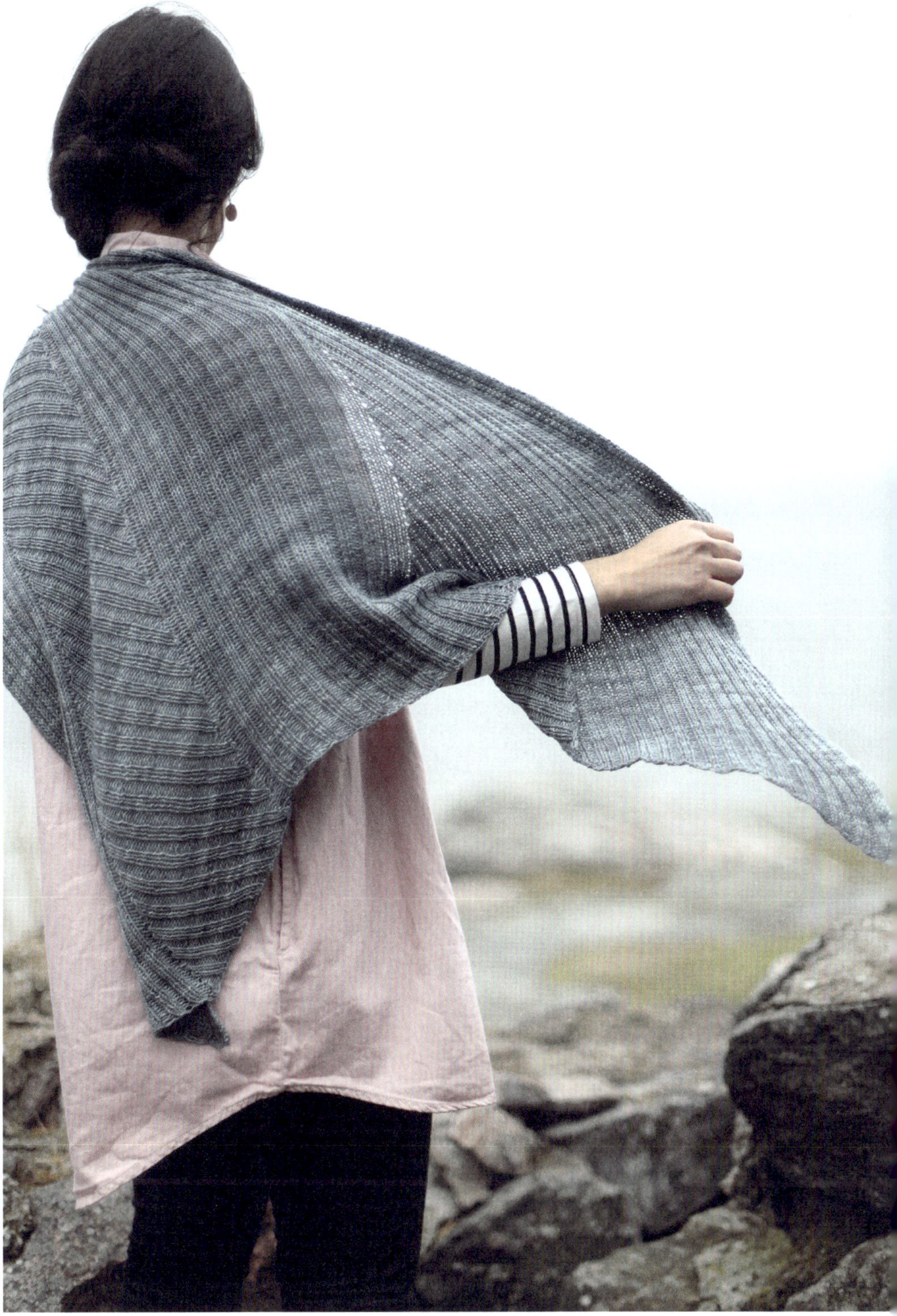

focus

ley lines shawls

true friend sweater

ley lines
by joji locatelli

It is amazing how our focus shifts in the most random ways and, like happened with this design, it often takes us to a very creative place when we let it wander around. The ribbing in this shawl will let your imagination and attention wander around too while you work its very simple instructions, and will leave you amazed at the direction your knitting took when you bind off the last remaining stitch.

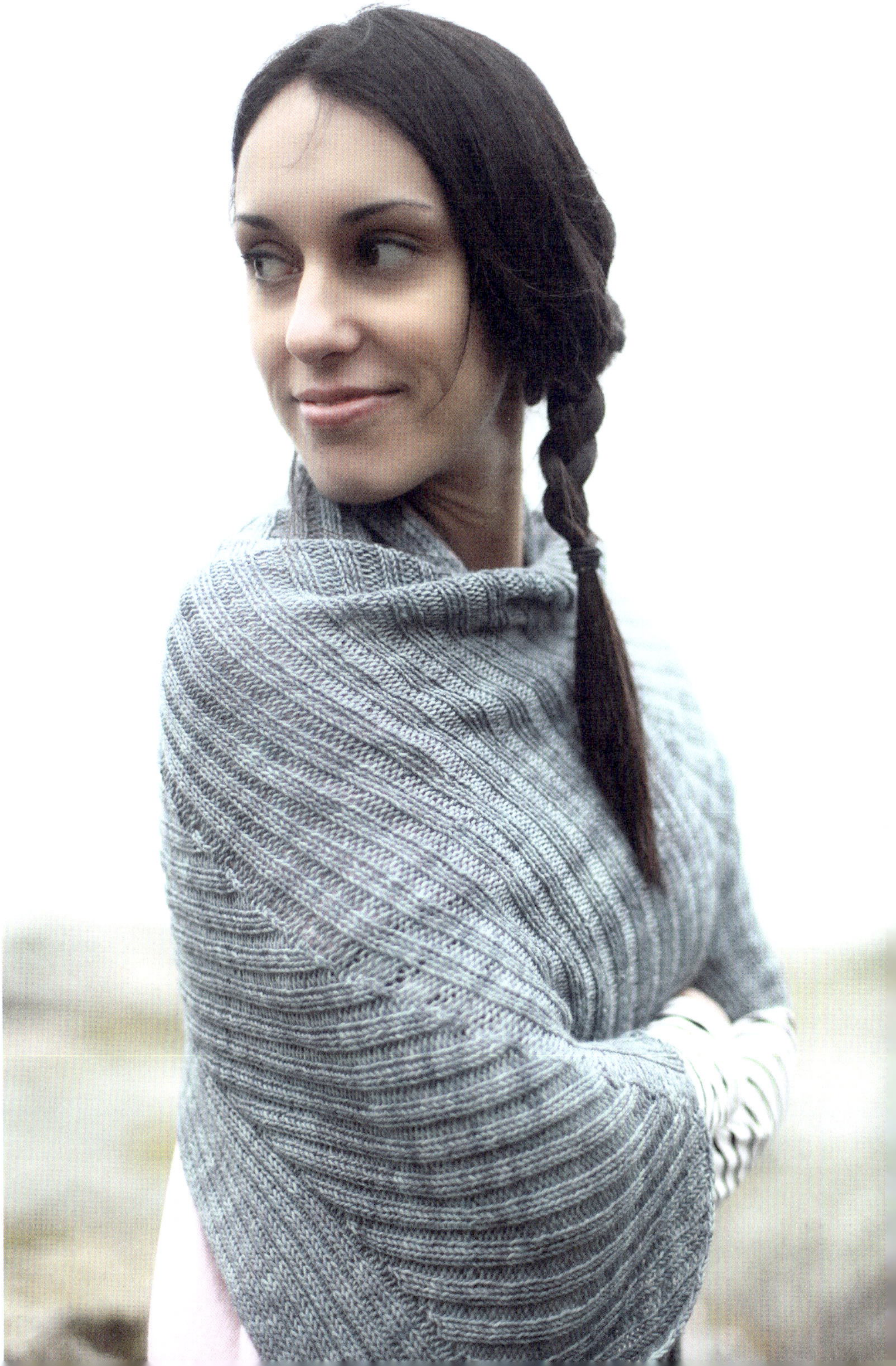

ley lines

Sizes

One size.

Finished measurements: 90" (225 cm) from side to side and 34" (85 cm) from top to bottom at deepest point.

Materials

Yarn: 2 skeins of Pure by Wollmeise (100% merino; 575 yd [526 m] - 150g). Approx. 950 yd [869 m] of fingering weight yarn. The sample was knit using the colorway Montblanc.
Needles: US 5 (3.75 mm) needles.
Other: Stitch markers, row counter (optional), blocking aids.

Gauge

22 stitches and 30 rows = 4" (10 cm) in 2x2 ribbing slightly stretched on US 5 (3.75 mm) needles.

Finished Measurements

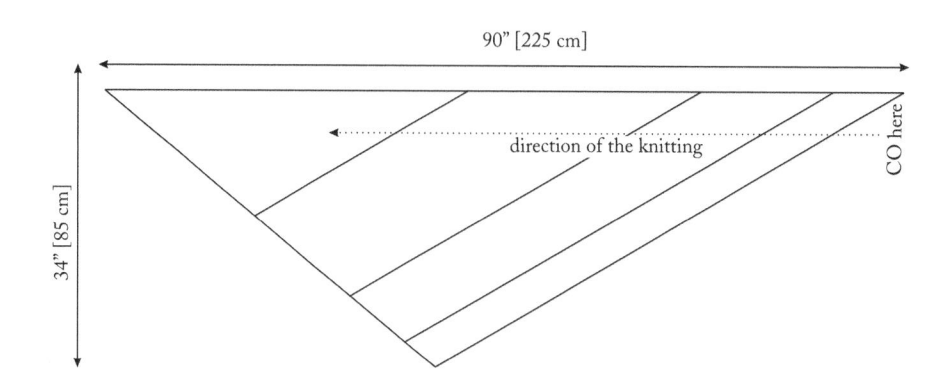

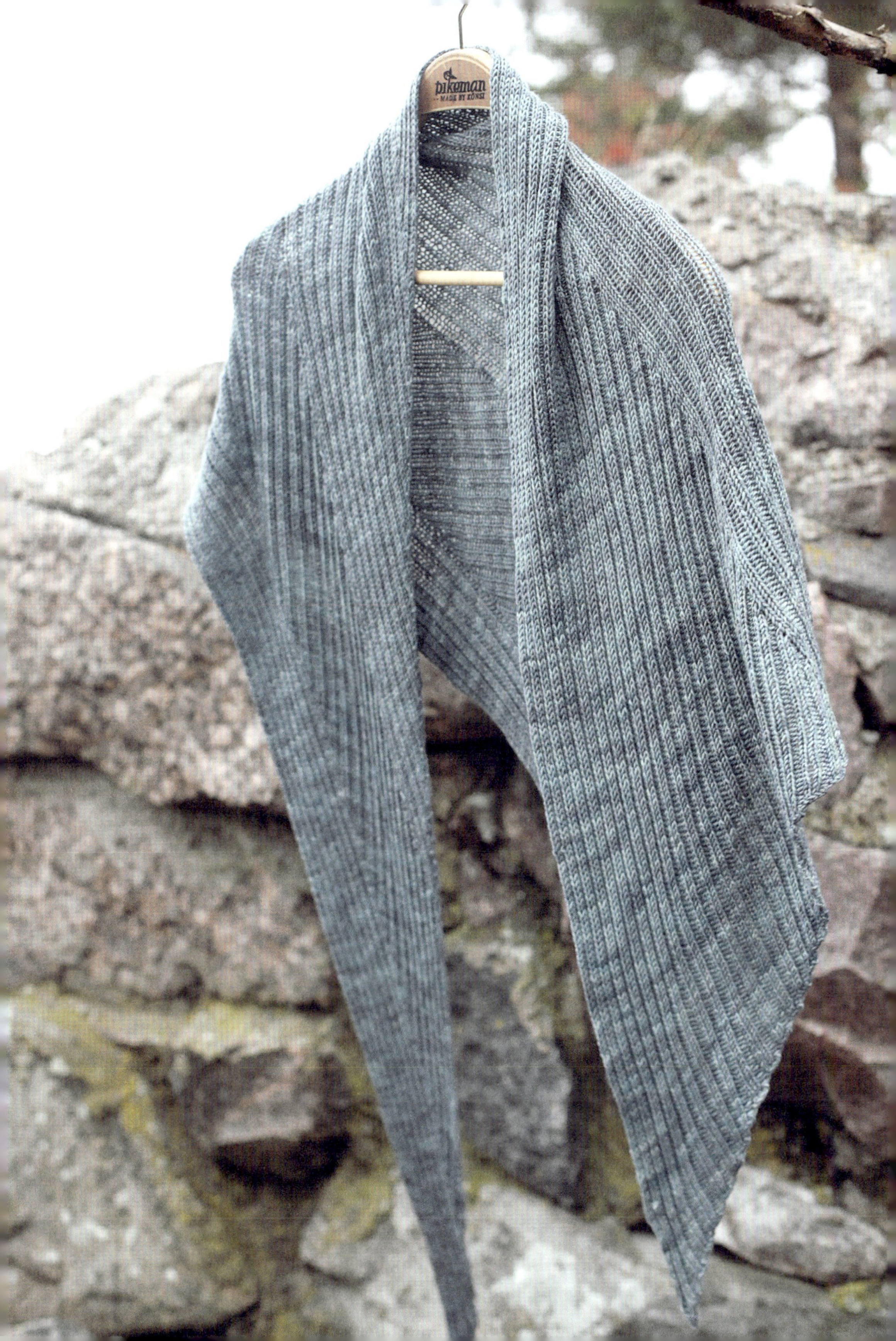

ley lines

Directions

CO 3 st.
Set-up row: P2, k1.

Section 1

Row 1: P1, m1p, k2.
Row 2 and all even-numbered rows: Work st as they appear (knit the knit st and purl the purl st).
Row 3: K1, m1p, p1, k2. (*5 st*)
Row 5: K1, m1R, (p2, k2) to end. (*6 st*)
Row 7: K1, m1R, k1, (p2, k2) to end. (*7 st*)
Row 9: P1, m1p, k2, (p2, k2) to end. (*8 st*)
Row 11: K1, m1p, p1, k2, (p2, k2) to end. (*9 st*)
Repeat *rows 5-12* - 5 more times (*you should have 29 st*). Work *rows 5-6* once more (*30 st*).

Section 2

Row 1: Kfb, k1, (p2, k2) to end of row. (*31 st*)
Row 2 and all even-numbered rows: Work st as they appear.
Row 3: K1, m1R, pm, k2, (p2, k2) to end of row. (*32 st*)
Row 5: K2, m1p, sm, work in patt to end. (*33 st*)
Row 7: K2, p1, m1p, sm, work in patt to end. (*34 st*)

Row 9: (K2, p2) to m, m1R, sm, work in patt to end. (*35 st*)
Row 11: (K2, p2) to 1 st from m, k1, m1R, sm, work in patt to end. (*36 st*)
Row 13: K2, (p2, k2) to m, m1p, sm, work in patt to end. (*37 st*)
Row 15: K2, (p2, k2) to 1 st from m, p1, m1p, sm, work in patt to end. (*38 st*)
Work *rows 9-16* seven more times. *You should have 66 st.*

Section 3

Row 1: K1, pm, k1, (p2, k2) to 2 st from m, p2, m1R, sm, work in patt to end.
Row 2 and all even-numbered rows: Work st as they appear (slipping markers).
Row 3: K1, m1R, sm, p2tog, p1, (k2, p2) to 1 st from m, k1, m1R, sm, work in patt to end.
Row 5: K1, m1R, k1, sm, p2tog, (k2, p2) to 2 st from m, k2, m1p, sm, work in patt to end.

64

Row 7: P1, m1p, k2, sm, k2tog, k1, (p2, k2) to 1 st from m, p1, m1p, sm, work in patt to end.
Row 9: K1, m1p, p1, k2, sm, k2tog, p2, (k2, p2) to m, m1R, sm, work in patt to end.
Row 11: K1, m1R, (p2, k2) to m, sm, p2tog, p1, (k2, p2) to 1 st from m, k1, m1R, sm, work in patt to end.
Row 13: K1, m1R, k1, (p2, k2) to m, sm, p2tog, k2, (p2, k2) to m, m1R, sm, work in patt to end.
Row 15: P1, m1p, k2, (p2, k2) to m, sm, k2tog, k1, (p2, k2) to 1 st from m, p1, m1p, sm, work in patt to end.
Row 17: K1, m1p, p1, k2, (p2, k2) to m, sm, k2tog, p2, (k2, p2) to m, m1R, sm, work in patt to end.

Work *rows 11-18* nine more times, and then *rows 11-12* once more. *You should have 112 st.*

Section 4

Row 1: Kfb, k1, (p2, k2) to m, sm, p2tog, (k2, p2) to 2 st from next m, k2, m1p, sm, k2, (p2, k2) to end.
Row 2 and all foll even-numbered rows: Work all st as they appear.
Row 3: K1, m1R, pm, k2, (p2, k2) to m, sm, k2tog, k1, (p2, k2) to 1 st from m, p1, m1p, sm, work in patt to end.
Row 5: K2, m1p, sm, k2, (p2, k2) to m, sm, k2tog, (p2, k2) to 2 st from m, p2, m1R, sm, work in patt to end.
Row 7: K2, p1, m1p, sm, k2, (p2, k2) to m, sm, p2tog, p1 (k2, p2) to 1 st from m, k1, m1R, sm, work in patt to end.
Row 9: (K2, p2) to m, m1R, sm, work in patt to next m, sm, p2tog, (k2, p2) to 2 st from m, k2, m1p, sm, work in patt to end.
Row 11: (K2, p2) to 1 st from m, k1, m1R, sm, work in patt to next m, sm, k2tog, k1, (p2, k2) to 1 st from m, p1, m1p, sm, work in patt to end.

Row 13: K2, (p2, k2) to m, m1p, sm, work in patt to next m, sm, k2tog, (p2, k2) to 2 st from m, p2, m1R, sm, work in patt to end.
Row 15: K2, (p2, k2) to 1 st from m, p1, m1p, sm, work in patt to next m, sm, p2tog, p1 (k2, p2) to 1 st from m, k1, m1R, sm, work in patt to end.

Work *rows 9- 16* 18 more times (*you should have 80 st between the beginning of the row and 1st marker*).

The next section is the section where you finish your shawl by binding off your stitches while still working in pattern. If you wish to make the shawl slightly smaller or larger, you can work fewer or more repeats of *rows 9-16*, and then move to Section 5.

Section 5

In this section, continue to work in pattern the same as you did for Section 4 (including all increases and decreases), but replace the even numbered rows for:

Row 2 and all foll even-numbered rows: P2tog, BO 3 st in pattern, work the rest of the st as they appear (k the k and p the p).

As you gradually work, you will bind off all the st from the different sections, just keep working to the end of your rows in pattern, binding off on the even rows.

Work in this manner until you have bound off all your stitches.

Finishing

Soak shawl and block gently to finished measurements.

true friend

by veera välimäki

Here and there, going back and forth, going up and down; this sweater focuses on a new construction and striping that makes the construction even more visible. Focus your senses and see a new lovely sweater form on your needles! Completely seamless, this sweater is fun to knit and super comfortable to wear.

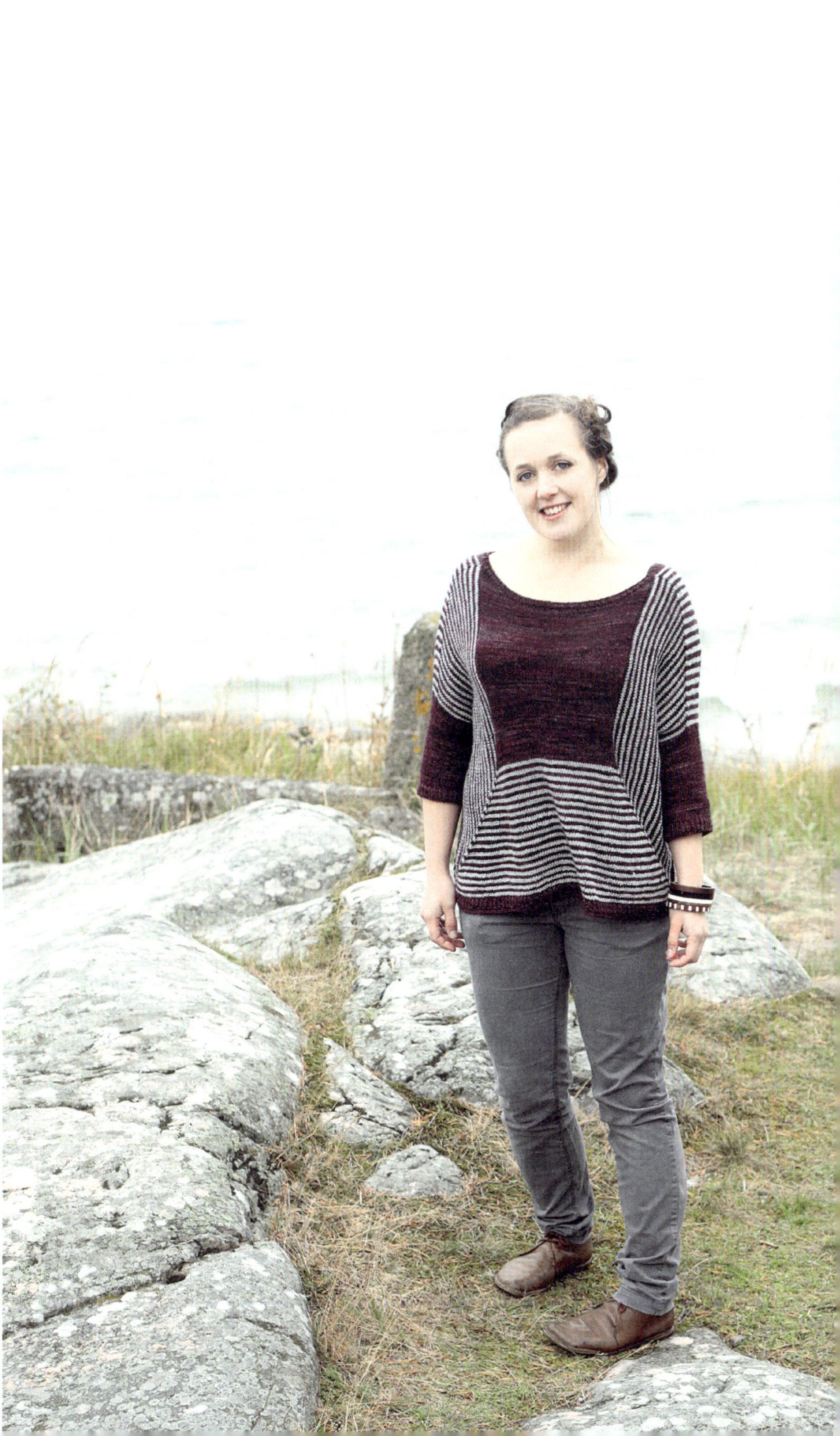

true friend

Sizes

XS (S, M, L, XL, XXL), shown in size S.
Finished chest circumference: 39½ (43½, 47½, 51½, 56½, 60½)" [98 (108, 118, 128, 142, 152) cm]. Choose a size with approx. 9" [23 cm] of positive ease.

Materials

Yarn: 3 (3, 4, 5, 5, 5) skeins of Tosh Merino Light by Madelinetosh (100% merino; 420 yd [384 m] - 100 g skein); 2 (2, 3, 3, 3, 3) skeins of MC and 1 (1, 1, 2, 2, 2) skeins of CC. Approx. 1120 (1240, 1400, 1540, 1700, 1900) yd [1025 (1135, 1280, 1410, 1555, 1740) m] of fingering weight yarn. The sample was knit in colorways Duchess (MC, purple) and Smokestack (CC, grey).

Needles: US 4 [3.5 mm] and US 2½ [3 mm] circular needle, 32" [80 cm] long, and dpns. Adjust needle size if necessary to obtain the correct gauge.

Other: Stitch markers, stitch holders / waste yarn, tapestry needle and blocking aids.

Gauge

24 stitches and 32 rows = 4" [10 cm] in Stockinette stitch, using larger needle.

Finished Measurements

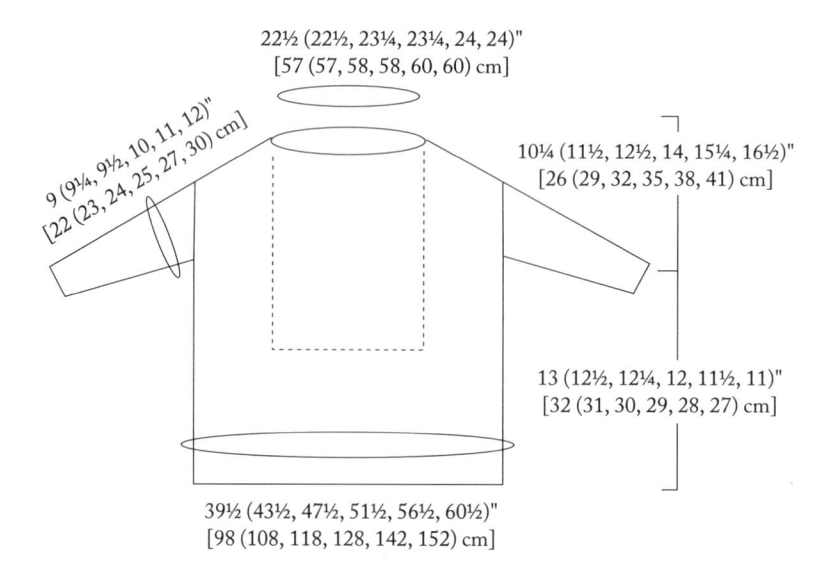

22½ (22½, 23¼, 23¼, 24, 24)"
[57 (57, 58, 58, 60, 60) cm]

9 (9¼, 9½, 10, 11, 12)"
[22 (23, 24, 25, 27, 30) cm]

10¼ (11½, 12½, 14, 15¼, 16½)"
[26 (29, 32, 35, 38, 41) cm]

13 (12½, 12¼, 12, 11½, 11)"
[32 (31, 30, 29, 28, 27) cm]

39½ (43½, 47½, 51½, 56½, 60½)"
[98 (108, 118, 128, 142, 152) cm]

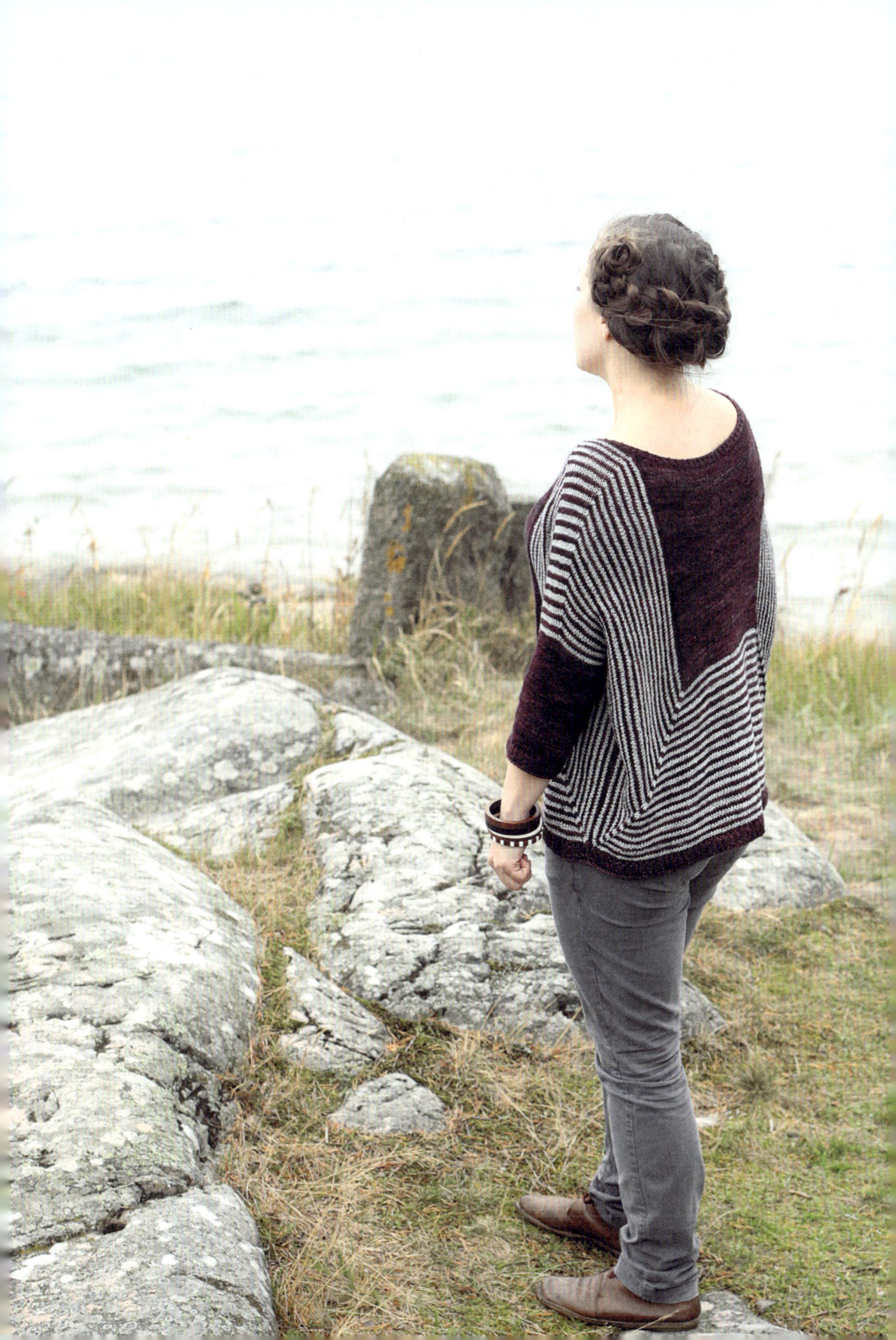

true friend

Collar

Using smaller circular needle and MC, CO 136 (136, 140, 140, 144, 144) sts. Pm for beginning of round and join carefully, not twisting your stitches. Knit one round and work 5 rounds in twisted ribbing (*k1 tbl, p1; rep from * to end of round*).

Front of the body

Note: you now have all the collar stitches on one circular needle, but work only the front stitches (back and forth). You can place all the stitches on larger circular first if that makes knitting easier.

Change to larger circ needle, sm and knit 5 (5, 6, 6, 7, 7) stitches (these stitches remain for shoulder), pm for beginning of front piece. Begin short row shaping of the front as follows:

Short row 1 (RS): Knit 2, turn work.

Short row 2 (WS): Yo, p2, turn work.

Short row 3 (RS): Knit to previous yo, k2tog the yarn over with the next stitch, k1, turn work.

Short row 4 (WS): Yo, purl to marker, turn work.

Repeat *short rows 3 and 4* – four times more. Work to end of front: Knit to previous yo, k2tog the yarn over with the next stitch, k45, pm for the end of the front piece (*note: you can remove this marker as soon as the turning point is clear to see*) and turn work.

Work the short rows from other side of the front:

Short row 5 (WS): Purl 2, turn work.

Short row 6 (RS): Yo, k2, turn work.

Short row 7 (WS): Purl to previous yo, ssp the yarn over with the next stitch, p1, turn work.

Short row 8 (RS): Yo, knit to marker, turn work.

Repeat *short rows 7 and 8* – four times more. Work to end of front: Purl to previous yo, ssp the yarn over with the next stitch, purl 45 to the end of the front piece and turn work.

Continue even with the 58 stitches of the front using MC. Work back and forth in St st until the piece measures 13 (12¾, 12¼, 12, 11½, 11)" [33 (32, 31, 30, 29, 28) cm], ending with a RS row. Leave stitches on needle and cut yarn.

Back of the body

Re-attach yarn to stitches after the long front piece. Knit 10 (10, 12, 12, 14, 14) and pm for beginning of back piece (*note: you can remove this marker as soon as the turning point is clear to see*). Begin short row shaping of the back as follows:

Short row 9 (RS): Knit 2, turn work.

Short row 10 (WS): Yo, p2, turn work.

Short row 11 (RS): Knit to previous yo, k2tog the yarn over with the next stitch, k1, turn work.

Short row 12 (WS): Yo, purl to marker, turn work.

Repeat *short rows 11 and 12* – once more. Work to end of front: Knit to previous yo, k2tog the yarn over with the next stitch, knit 51, pm for the end of the back piece and turn work.

Work the short rows from other side of the front:

Short row 13 (WS): Purl 2, turn work.

Short row 14 (RS): Yo, k2, turn work.

Short row 15 (WS): Purl to previous yo, ssp the yarn over with the next stitch, p1, turn work.

Short row 16 (RS): Yo, knit to marker, turn work.

Repeat *short rows 15 and 16* – once more. Work to end of front: Purl to previous yo, ssp the yarn-over with the next stitch, purl 51 to the end of the back piece and turn work.

Continue even with the 58 stitches of the back using MC. Work back and forth in St st until the piece measures 13 (12¾, 12¼, 12, 11½, 11)" [33 (32, 31, 30, 29, 28) cm], ending with a RS row. Leave stitches on needle and keep yarn attached.

Striped part of body

Place marker for the new beginning of round and pick up stitches for the body on first round –

Next round (RS): With RS of the back piece facing, pick up and knit 80 stitches up the right side long edge of back piece to marker, sm, knit 5 (5, 6, 6, 7, 7) stitches to first beg of rnd marker, remove marker and knit 5 (5, 6, 6, 7, 7) stitches to next m, sm, pick up and knit 80 stitches down the right side long edge of front piece to front stitches on needle, pm, knit 58 sts of front, pm, pick up and knit 80 stitches up the left side long edge of the front piece to marker, sm, knit 10 (10, 12, 12, 14, 14) shoulder stitches to m, sm, pick up and knit 80 stitches down the left side long edge of the back piece to back stitches on needle, pm, knit 58 sts of back to end of round. [*456 (456, 460, 460, 464, 464) sts on needle.*]

Continue working in the round and begin striping and **at the same time** increases and decreases to shape the body –

Round 1 (MC, increase): *Sm, k1, m1L, k until 2 stitches before m remain, k2tog, sm, k to m, sm, ssk, k until 1 st before m remain, m1R, k1, sm, k1, m1L, k until 1 st before m remain, m1R, k1; repeat once from *.

Round 2 (MC): Knit to end slipping all markers.

Round 3 (CC, increase): *Sm, k1, m1L, k until 2 stitches before m remain, k2tog, sm, k to m, sm, ssk, k until 1 st before m remain, m1R, k1, sm, k1, m1L, k until 1 st before m remain, m1R, k1; repeat once from *.

Round 4 (CC): Knit to end slipping all markers.

Repeat **rounds 1 to 4** – 14 (17, 20, 23, 27, 30) times more. Knit **rounds 1 and 2** once more and continue with MC. [*580 (604, 632, 656, 692, 716) sts on needle.*]

BO side seams with three-needle bind-off on next round – *Note: remove all markers.*

Next round (RS): Sm, knit until 20 (21, 21, 22, 23, 26) sts before marker remain, place the next 50 (52, 54, 56, 60, 66) sts on holder for sleeve and remove the two markers in sleeve stitches, turn the piece inside out (now WS facing) and BO the remaining 60 (59, 59, 58, 57, 54) side sts using three-needle BO working your way down to body stitches, keep yarn attached and decrease the last remaining stitch from the BO and then knit the 120 (132, 144, 156, 172, 184) sts of front, sm, knit until 20 (21, 21, 22, 23, 26) sts before marker remain, place the next 50 (52, 54, 56, 60, 66) sts on holder for sleeve and remove the two markers in sleeve stitches, turn the piece inside out (now WS facing) and BO the remaining 60 (59, 59, 58, 57, 54) side sts using three-needle BO working your way down to body stitches, keep yarn attached and decrease the last remaining stitch from the BO and then knit the 120 (132, 144, 156, 172, 184) sts of back to end of round.

Continue with the 240 (264, 288, 312, 344, 368) stitches on needle and MC. Change to smaller circular needle and pm for beginning of round. Work 1" [2.5 cm] in twisted ribbing. Knit one round. BO stitches loosely on next round.

Sleeves

Place held stitches on dpns and pick up 4 (4, 4, 4, 6, 6) stitches from the underarm. Join MC to underarm (center of the picked up stitches), pm to beg of round and work in St st.

Decrease twice every 2" [5 cm]: Sm, k2, ssk, k until 4 stitches before m remain, k2tog, k2.

When sleeve measures 6½" [16 cm], change to smaller dpns and work 1" [2.5 cm] in twisted ribbing. Knit one round. BO stitches loosely on next round.

Finishing

Weave in ends and block garment to finished measurements.

quiet

There are some who would wake up early (on purpose, who knew right?), before the rest of the family, to enjoy that special quiet that morning brings. Sometimes quiet is the most relaxed feeling you can get. It offers silence of the mind and a way to find clarity. When you are quiet enough, you can hear wonderful things.

As knitters, we enjoy the quiet in our projects, with subtle details, quiet shapes, meditative patterns that offer peace to our stressed souls. We also love these quiet moments to dive into a pattern and open up a whole new kind of noise, those of our needles clicking as we knit our little hearts out.

Enjoy the quiet.

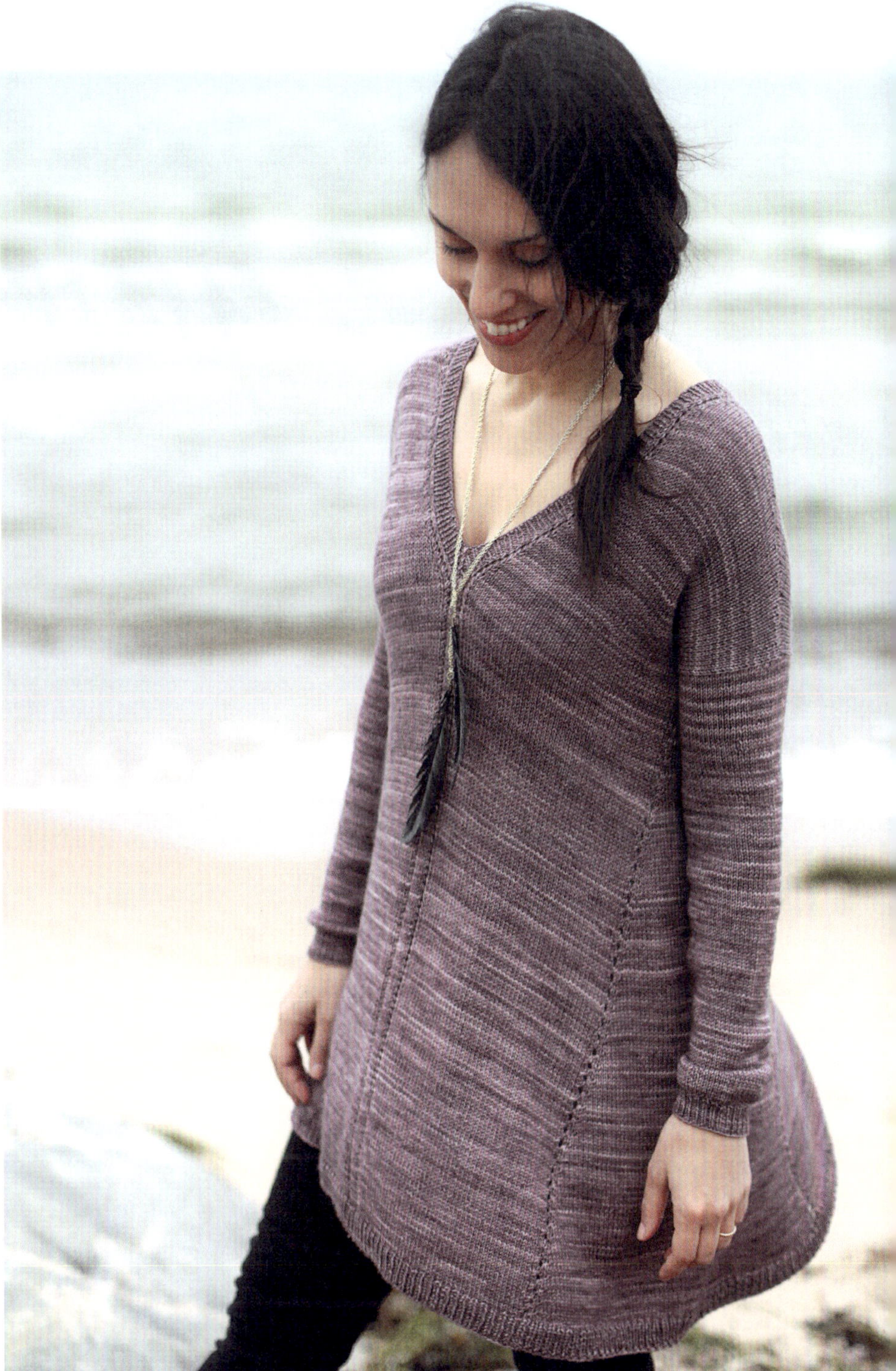

quiet

serenity sweater

above the horizon beanie

serenity
by joji locatelli

As women and knitters, we long for serenity, peace of mind...
We look for projects that don't require us to be fully focused, but we also constantly wish for garments that will make us look good. This design brings you lots of mindless knitting with enough details to keep you motivated. Clean lines, draped fabric and a flattering A-line shape are the key points in this feminine tunic. The V-neck adds a bit of flirt if you are in the mood for it.
It will make you feel confident, beautiful, at peace with yourself.

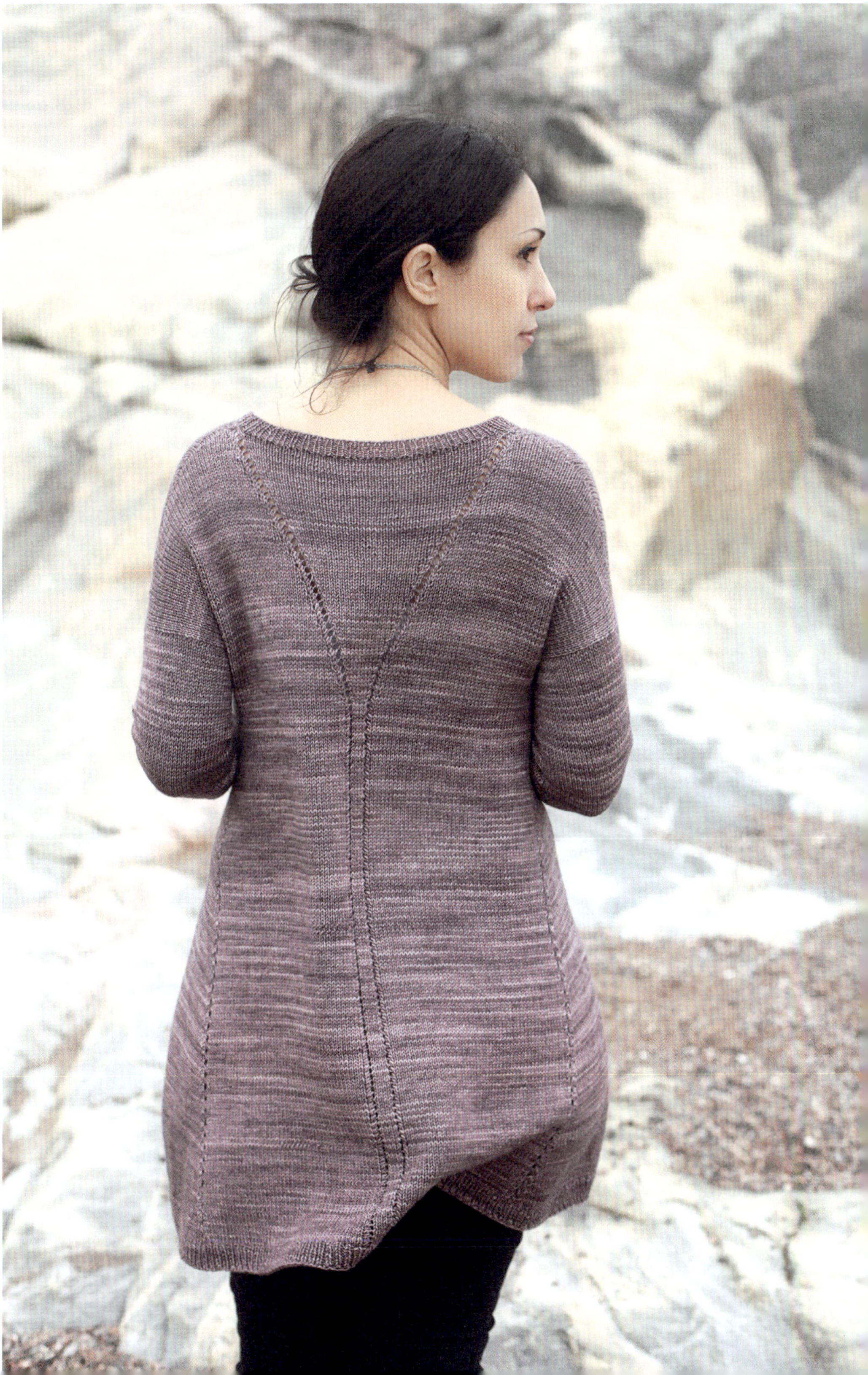

serenity

Sizes

XS (S, M, L, XL, XXL, 3XL), shown in size M (recommended ease: +2-3" [5-8 cm]).

Finished measurements
Bust circumference: 33 (35, 39, 42, 47, 51, 55)" [83 (88, 98, 108, 128, 138) cm].
Bottom circumference at hem: 62½ (64, 68, 72¼, 76½, 80½, 84¼)" [156 (160, 170, 181, 191, 202, 210) cm].
Mid-upper arm circumference: 10 (11¼, 12, 13¼, 14, 15¼, 16¾)" [25 (28, 30, 33, 35, 38, 42) cm].
Sleeve length from underarm to cuff: 17" [42½ cm].
Length from underarm to hem (after blocking): 23" [58 cm].

Materials

Yarn: 4 (5, 5, 5, 6, 6, 7) skeins of Primo Fingering by The Plucky Knitter (70% merino, 25% cashmere, 10% nylon; 390 yd [357 m] - 100 g). Approx 1500 (1650, 1750, 1880, 2050, 2200, 2500) yd [1372 (1509, 1600, 1719, 1875, 2012, 2286) m] of fingering weight yarn. The sample was knit in size M using the P's and Q's colorway.
Needles: US 4 [3.5 mm] and US 2½ [3 mm] circular needles; crochet hook for provisional cast on.
Other: Stitch markers, 4 safety pins to use as stitch holders, stitch holders, waste yarn.

Gauge

23 st and 34 rows = 4" [10 cm], on US 4 [3.5 mm] needles in Stockinette stitch, after blocking.

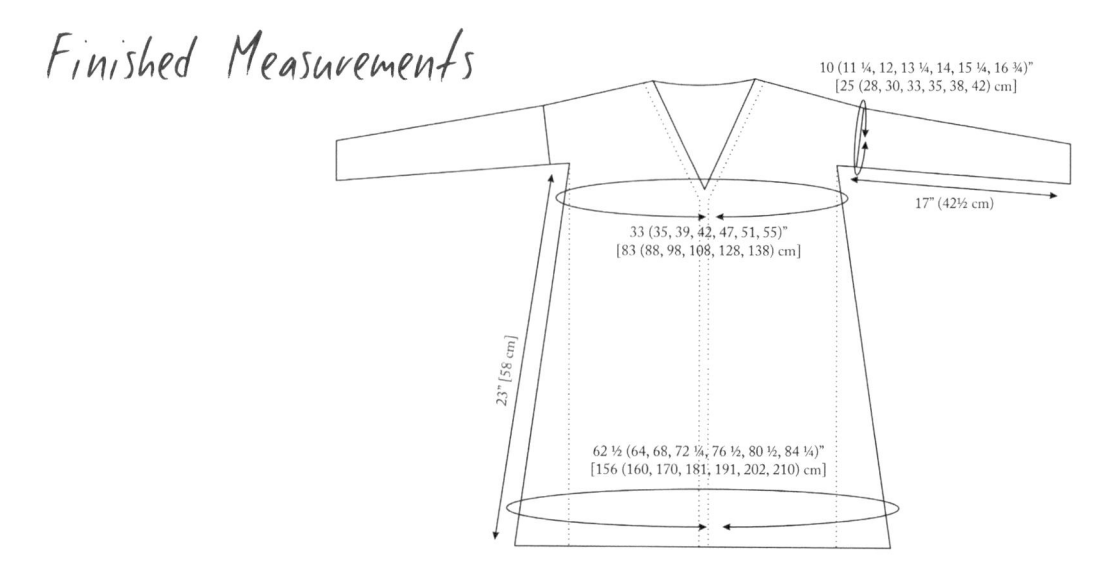

Finished Measurements

10 (11 ¼, 12, 13 ¼, 14, 15 ¼, 16 ¾)" [25 (28, 30, 33, 35, 38, 42) cm]

17" (42½ cm)

33 (35, 39, 42, 47, 51, 55)" [83 (88, 98, 108, 128, 138) cm]

23" [58 cm]

62 ½ (64, 68, 72 ¼, 76 ½, 80 ½, 84 ¼)" [156 (160, 170, 181, 191, 202, 210) cm]

serenity

Right Back Shoulder

With waste yarn and using your US 4 [3.5 mm] needles, provisionally cast on 34 (36, 40, 45, 48, 54, 57) st.

Set-up row: P to end of row.

Row 1 (RS): K3, pm, yo, ssk, k1, W&T.

Row 2 (WS): P to end.

Row 3: K1, k2tog, sm, yo, ssk, m1R, k to wrapped st, knit it with wrap, k3, W&T.

Row 4: P to end.

Break yarn and put on hold.

Left Back Shoulder

Provisionally CO 34 (36, 40, 45, 48, 54, 57) st.

Set-up Row: P to end of row.

Row 1 (RS): K to 5 st from end, k2tog, yo, pm, k3.

Row 2 (WS): P 6, W&T.

Row 3: K to 2 st before m, m1L, k2tog, yo, sm, ssk, k1.

Row 4: P to wrapped st and purl it tog with wrap, p3, W&T.

Join Back Shoulders

Row 1 (RS): K to 2 st from m, k2tog, yo, sm, k2, CO 36 (36, 40, 42, 48, 48, 52) st. Place the held st from the other shoulder on the needles. K to m, sm, yo, ssk, k to last wrapped st, knit it with wrap, k3, W&T. *You should have: 104 (108, 120, 132, 144, 156, 166) st distributed the foll way: 32 (34, 38, 43, 46, 52, 55) st at the shoulders and 40 (40, 44, 46, 52, 52, 56) st at the center, between the markers.*

Row 2 (WS): P to last wrapped st, purl it tog with wrap, p3, W&T.

Row 3: K to 2 st from m, m1L, k2tog, yo, sm, ssk, k to 2 st before next m, k2tog, sm, yo, ssk, m1R, k to last wrapped st and k it with wrap, k3, W&T.

Rows 4 and 6: Same as row 2.

Row 5: K to 2 st from m, k2tog, yo, sm, k to m, sm, yo, ssk, k to last wrapped st, and knit it with wrap, k3, W&T.

Repeat *rows 3-6* 1 (1, 2, 2, 3, 3, 3) more times.

Next row (RS): K to 2 st from m, m1L, k2tog, yo, sm, ssk, k to 2 st before next m, k2tog, sm, yo, ssk, m1R, k to the end of row, picking up wrap and knitting it with its corresponding st.

Next row (WS): P to end of row, picking up wrap and purling it with its corresponding st.

You should have the same st count, but now distributed the foll way: 35 (37, 42, 47, 51, 57, 60) st at each side of the markers, and 34 (34, 36, 38, 42, 42, 46) st at the center, between the markers.

Upper Back

Row 1 (RS): K to 2 st from m, k2tog, yo, sm, k to m, sm, yo, ssk, k to end of row.

Rows 2 and 4 (WS): Purl to end of row.

Row 3 (RS): K to 2 st from m, m1L, k2tog, yo, sm, ssk, k to 2 st before next m, k2tog, sm, yo, ssk, m1R, k to end.

Repeat *rows 1-4* until your piece measures 4½ (4¾, 5¼, 5½, 6¾, 7¼, 8)" [11 (12, 13, 14, 17, 18, 20) cm] from your CO edge, measured along the side of the garment (the armhole edge), ending with row 2 of your repeat. *Take note of the number of repeats you work here because you will have to work the fronts to an equal number of repeats.*

Break yarn and put on hold, transferring markers too.

A note about what's happening in the back

As you must have noticed by now, the eyelets get closer and closer as you work repeats. The tunic is designed so that when you join in the round, all the eyelets match and you only have 4 stitches between the eyelets both in the front and in the back (this should happen AFTER you join the body, and exactly WHEN you join the fronts).

It might happen that you want to make the armhole deeper, or that your row gauge is slightly tighter or looser... or that you missed an increase here or there! This will make things work differently, but it's easy to solve. When your eyelets on the back are 4 st apart, stop working the increase/decrease described on row 3, and just continue to work the eyelets down without moving them (this is achieved by just repeating Rows 1-2).

Right Front

Unravel the provisional st for the Right Shoulder and place them on the needle, ready to start a RS row. Place a split ring st marker here, so you can identify the point where you rejoined your yarn.

Row 1 (RS): K to 4 st from end, k2tog, yo, k2.

Row 2 (WS): P5, W&T.

Row 3: K to 4 st from end, m1L, k2tog, yo, k2.

Rows 4, 6: P to last wrapped st and p it with wrap, p3, W&T

Row 5: K to 4 st from end, k2tog, yo, k2.

Work *rows 3-6* - 2 (2, 3, 3, 4, 4, 4) more times.

Next row (RS): K to 4 st from end, m1L, k2tog, yo, k2.

Next row (WS): P to last wrapped st and p it with wrap, p to end.

Start front pattern

Row 1 (RS): K to 4 st from end, k2tog, yo, k2.

Rows 2 and 4 (WS): P to end.

Row 3: K to 4 st from end, m1L, k2tog, yo, k2.

Repeat these 4 rows until your work measures 4½ (4¾, 5¼, 5½, 6¾, 7¼, 8)" [11 (12, 13, 14, 17, 18, 20) cm] from the point where you picked up your stitches, ending with *row 2* of your repeat. You should work the same amount of repeats as you did for your back, so that the eyelet placement matches in both sides.

Break yarn and put all st on hold.

Left Front

Unravel the provisional st for the Left Shoulder and place them on the needle, ready to start a RS row.

Row 1 (RS): K2, yo, ssk, k1, W&T.

Rows 2, 4 (WS): P to end.

Row 3: K2, yo, ssk, m1R, k to last wrapped st and k it with wrap, k3, W&T.

Row 5: K2, yo, ssk, k to last wrapped st and k it with wrap, k3, W&T.

Row 6: P to end.

Work *rows 3-6* - 2 (2, 3, 3, 4, 4, 4) more times.

Next row (RS): K2, yo, ssk, m1R, k to last wrapped st and k it with wrap, k to end of row.

Next row (WS): P to end.

Start front pattern

Row 1 (RS): K2, yo, ssk, k to end.

Rows 2 and 4: P to end.

Row 3: K2, yo, ssk, m1R, k to end.

Repeat these 4 rows until your work measures 4½ (4¾, 5¼, 5½, 6¾, 7¼, 8)" [11 (12, 13, 14, 17, 18, 20) cm] from the point where you picked up your stitches, ending with *row 2* of your repeat (work the same number of repeats as you did for the Back and Right Front).

Join Body

Starting with the foll RS row and with the Left Front stitches: K2, yo, ssk, m1R, k to 4 st before the end and put these 4 remaining st on hold using a safety pin.

Transfer all the st you had on hold for the Back onto the needles (transferring markers too). Put the first 4 st on hold using another safety pin and work as follows: Pm, knit to 2 st before m, m1L, k2tog, yo, sm, ssk, k to 2 st from next m, k2tog, sm, yo, ssk, m1R, k to 4 st before the end of row, put 4 st on hold.

Transfer all the st you had on hold for the Right Front onto the needles. Put the first 4 st on hold. Pm, k to 4 st from end, m1L, k2tog, yo, k2. Turn work. Leave all the st you have on the safety pins on hold.

Your front pieces (now on the needle with the back) will have a variable st count depending on how many times you have worked the repeat so far, and the back piece should now have 96 (100, 112, 124, 136, 148, 158) st.

Next row (WS): P to end.

Row 1 (RS): K2, yo, ssk, k to 2 st before 2nd foll m, k2tog, yo, sm, k to next m, sm, yo, ssk, k to 4 st from end, k2tog, yo, k2.

Rows 2 and 4 (WS): P to end.

Row 3: K2, yo, ssk, m1R, k to 2 st before 2nd foll m, m1L, k2tog, yo, sm, ssk, k to 2 st before next m, k2tog, sm, yo, ssk, m1R, k to 4 st from end, m1L, k2tog, yo, k2.

Repeat *rows 1-4* until you have 48 (50, 56, 62, 68, 74, 79) st for each front (excluding the st on safety pins), ending with *row 4* of your repeat.

Next row (RS) - Join for working in the round and re-arrange markers: K2, yo, ssk, k to 3 st before m, pm, k3, remove m, k3, pm, k to 2 st before next m, k2tog, yo, remove m, k2, pm, k2, remove m, yo, ssk, k to 3 st before next m, pm, k3, remove m, k3, pm, k to 4 st before end of round, k2tog, yo, k2, pm (beg of round). You should have 192 (200, 224, 248, 272, 296, 316) st on the needles.

Next round: K to end.

Start body shaping

Round 1: *k2, yo, ssk, k to 2 st before next m, k2tog, yo, sm, k1, m1R, k to 1 st from next m, m1L, k1, sm, yo, ssk, k to 4 st before next m, k2tog, yo, k2, sm; repeat from * once more. 4 st increased.

Rounds 2 and 4: K to end.

Round 3: *k2, yo, ssk, k to 4 st before the 3rd foll marker, k2tog, yo, k2, sm; repeat from * once more.

Repeat *rounds 1-4* until work measures 22" (55 cm) from the armhole (the garment will be blocked to be longer).

Note: The eyelets in the back and in the front happen every 2 rounds, and the eyelets on the side happen every 4 rounds.

Switch to US 2½ (3 mm) needles.

Work 8 rounds of k1, p1 ribbing, and on the following round BO all stitches loosely using an elastic bind-off (see Glossary).

Sleeves

Before starting the sleeves, graft the st you have on hold at the bottom of the armhole (4 st from the front together with 4 st from the back at each side).

With US 4 (3.5 mm) needles, pick up and knit 62 (68, 74, 80, 84, 92, 100) st around the armhole opening. Place marker at the beginning of the round.

Note: The sleeves are designed to be snug. If you want looser sleeves, you can pick up some more stitches in this section.

Work 8 (7, 6, 3, 1, 1, 1)" [20 (17½, 15, 7½, 2½, 2½, 2½ cm)] in Stockinette st.

Next round: knit to 2 st before marker, ssk, slip marker, k2tog (2 stitches decreased).

Continue working in Stockinette st repeating a decrease round every 8th (8th, 8th, 8th, 8th, 6th, 6th) round 6 (7, 8, 11, 13, 15, 17) more times. *You should have 48 (52, 56, 56, 56, 60, 64) st.*

Work in Stockinette st until sleeve measures 16"; 40 cm from the armhole. Switch to US 2½ (3 mm) needles.

Next round: *k1, p1*, repeat to the end of round.

Work 11 more rounds in ribbing and on the next round bind off all st in pattern.

Neckband

With smaller needle and starting at the back where it meets the left side, pick up and knit approx. 56 (56, 60, 60, 64, 64, 66) st along the left side of the neckline, pm, pick up 1 st from the center of the V-neck, pick up 56 (56, 60, 60, 64, 64, 66) st along the right side of the neckline, and 39 (39, 45, 45, 51, 51, 55) st along the back neck.

Round 1: (P1, k1) to 2 st before m, p1, sl 1 st to RN, remove m, move st back to LN, pm, sk2p, (p1, k1) to end of round.

Round 2: (P1, k1) to end of row.

Round 3: (P1, k1) to 1 st from m, sl 1 st to RN, remove m, move st back to LN, pm, sk2p, k1, (p1, k1) to end of round.

Round 4: (P1, k1) to m, sm, k2, (p1, k1) to end of round.

Work *rows 1-3* once more, and on the foll round bind off all st in pattern (do not use an elastic bind-off).

Finishing

Weave in ends and block sweater to measurements.

above the horizon

by veera välimäki

Above the Horizon is a fun little beanie that keeps you warm and toasty. Play with your two favorite colors, get going with a few rounds of simple colorwork and finish it up with some stripes. The hat is worked from bottom up and bound off at the top of the crown.

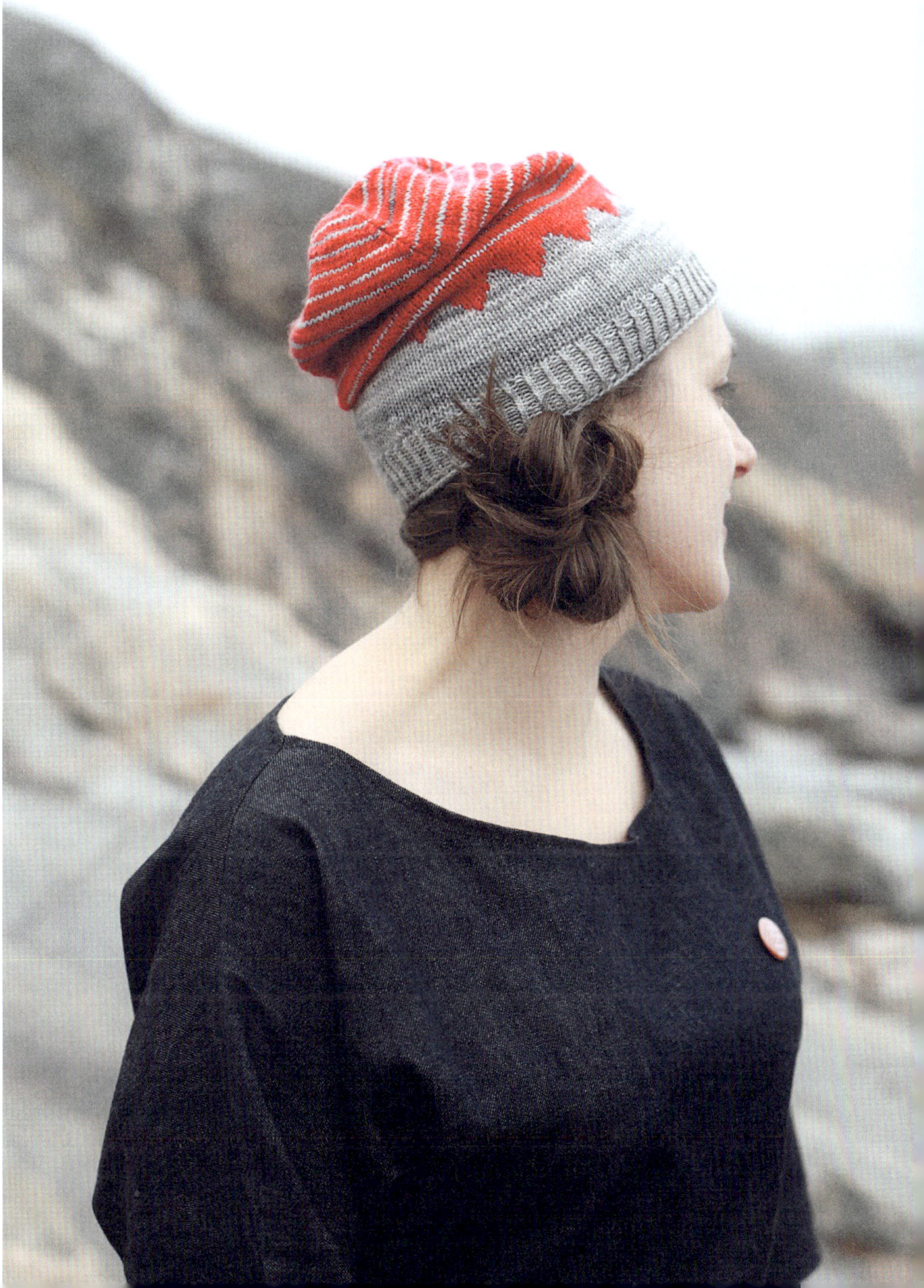

above the horizon

Sizes

S (L), shown in size S.
Finished brim circumference: 17 (19)" [42 (48) cm], unstretched.
Finished height: 8 (9)" [20 (23) cm].

Materials

Yarn: 2 skeins of Superwash Merino Fingering by Northbound Knitting (100% merino; 400 yd [366 m] - 100 g). Approx. 250 (290) yd [230 (265) m] of fingering weight yarn; one skein of MC and CC. The sample was knit in colorways Sterling (MC, grey) and Fiery (CC, red).
Needles: US 2½ [3 mm] and US 0 [2 mm] circular needles, 16" [40 cm] long or longer if using magic-loop method, and larger dpns. Adjust needle size if necessary to obtain the correct gauge.
Other: Stitch markers, tapestry needle and blocking aids.

Gauge

26 stitches and 36 rows = 4" [10 cm] in Stockinette stitch, using larger needle.

Finished Measurements

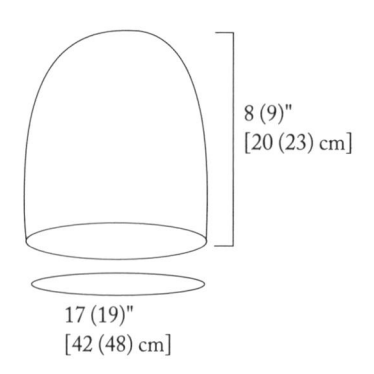

8 (9)"
[20 (23) cm]

17 (19)"
[42 (48) cm]

above the horizon

Brim

Using main color (MC) and smaller circular needle, CO 110 (124) sts. Carefully join in round, not twisting your stitches, and pm for beginning of round. Knit the first round, then continue 1¼" [3 cm] in twisted ribbing (*k1tbl, p1; repeat to end of round).

Body of the hat

Change to larger needle and continue in MC and St st. Increase on first round: Sm, *knit 11 (10), m1R; repeat 9 (11) times; knit to end if necessary in your size. [*You have 120 (136) sts on needle*]. Continue in St st using MC until the hat measures 3" [8 cm].

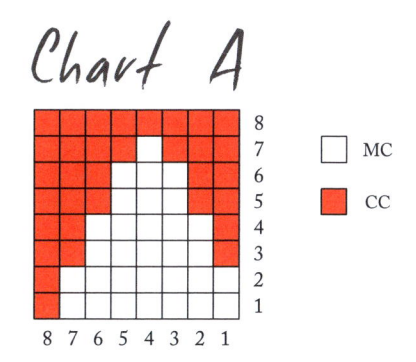

Chart A

	8	7	6	5	4	3	2	1

☐ MC
■ CC

Begin colorwork

Note: Catch the yarns every few sts by twisting the MC-CC yarns together to avoid long loops.

Round 1: Sm, work row 1 of chart A 15 (17) times (to end of round).

Round 2: Sm, work the next row of chart A 15 (17) times.

Continue repeating round 2 until all rows of chart A are worked.

Continue with striping

Work 3 rounds in CC, then 1 round in MC. Work striping until the beanie measures 6½ (7)" [17 (19) cm] from CO edge.

Crown decreases

Continue with striping and begin decreases as follows: Sm, *k2tog, k 26 (30), ssk, pm; repeat two times from *, k2tog, k 26 (30) to end of round. Knit one round.

Decrease round: *K2tog, k until two stitches before next m remain, ssk, sm; repeat three times from *.

Alternate decrease round and knit round (remember striping) until 40 stitches remain. *Note: change to dpns when necessary or work the beanie using magic loop technique.* Continue with CC only. When 16 stitches remain, cut yarn and thread through remaining stitches twice. Fasten securely.

Finishing

Weave in all yarn ends and block the hat using your preferred method.

charm

light pine woods whisper in your ear, saying the sweetest words. You can feel the sandy soil beneath your feet; feel the salt in the sea air. Everything you see is quiet and still, you can only hear the wind going through the woods. The light bounces from tree to tree, like a breeze, and you feel at ease. Everything is as it is supposed to be.

like an unexpected story, these designs unravel their charming secrets before your hands while you work on the knits. These designs show you the varied ways of enchanted elements that make them special, the playfulness of their nature.

87

charm

petites bulles beanie

state of mind cardigan

petites bulles
by joji locatelli

Simple things are easy to love. Wearing simple garments and accessories makes you feel light, transparent. We look at ourselves in the mirror and feel confident, elegant, minimalistic and modern. But sometimes, we need something else. Don't we? Because we also like to feel feminine, sweet, smart, graceful. We are women after all, and we need a little charm in our lives.

Like little droplets of dew, the bobbles on this simple beanie add just enough charm to your knitting to keep your inner girl feeling curious and charming as she always should.

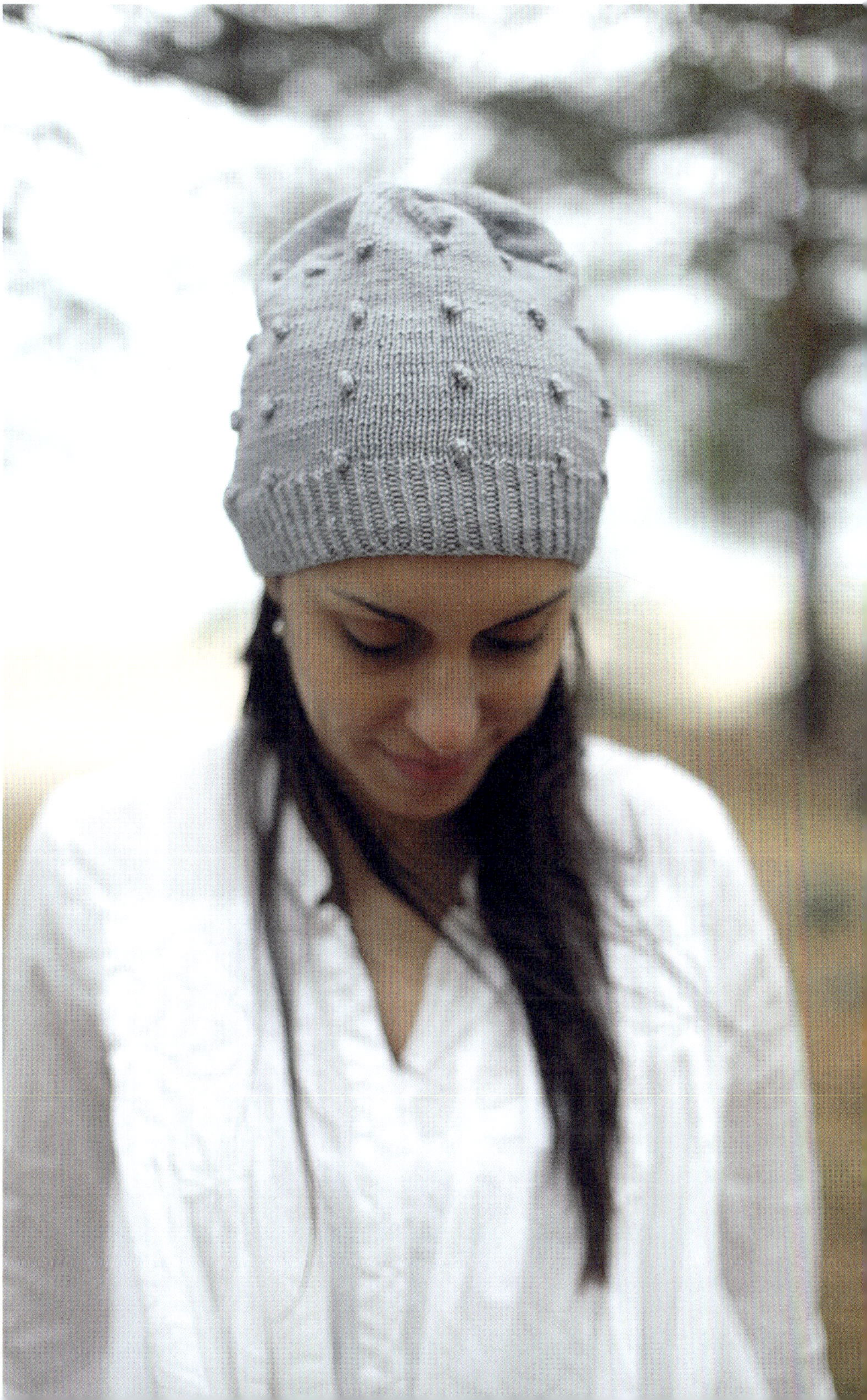

petites bulles

Sizes

M (L). Shown in size L.

Finished measurements: To fit average head circumference, 22" [56 cm], both sizes fully covering ears. The Large is 1¼" deeper, for a slouchy fit. For a tighter/looser fit, you can adjust the needle size you are going to use. Use 1 size smaller for a tighter fit and 1 size larger for a looser fit. Shown in size Large.

Materials

Yarn: 1 skein of King of the Jungle Merino Fingering by Lioness Arts (100% merino; 395 yd [361 m] - 100 g). Approx. 190 (220) yd [174 (201 m]of fingering weight yarn. The sample was knit in size L, in colorway Shapes in the Clouds.

Needles: US 2½ [3 mm] 16" [40 cm] circular needles and US 2½ [3 mm] dpn.

Other: Stitch marker, row counter (optional), tapestry needle.

Gauge

25 stitches and 36 rounds = 4" (10 cm) in Stockinette stitch on US 2½ (3 mm) needles.

Finished Measurements

19" (48 cm)

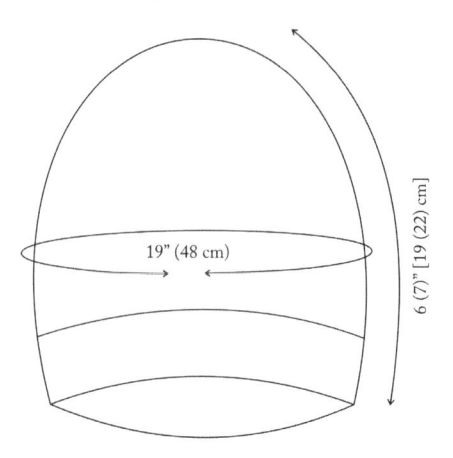

6 (7)" [19 (22) cm]

petites bulles

Directions

With US 2½ (3 mm) circular needles cast on 120 stitches and join for working in the round, placing a marker at the beginning.
Work in twisted rib (k1tbl, p1) for 18 rounds.

Next round: K all st.

Next round - Bobble round: K 30, pm, (MB, k9) 6 times, MB, k to end of round.

Knit 9 rounds.

Work another bobble round and keep knitting in the established pattern, working a bobble round every 10th round until you have worked a total of 4 bobble rounds (remove second marker after finishing last bobble round).

Continue working in Stockinette st until your hat measures 6" (7¼") [15 (18) cm] from your CO edge.

Crown decreases

Set-up round: *ssk, k16, k2tog, pm* 5 times, ssk, k16, k2tog. *108 st remain.*

Next round: K to end of round.

Decrease round: *ssk, k to 2 st before next m, k2tog, sm*; repeat to the end of round. *96 st remain.*

Next round: K to end of round.

Repeat the last 2 rounds 7 more times. *12 st remain.*

Finishing

Break yarn and draw through remaining stitches, pulling tightly. Sew it to the inside of the hat securely.

Weave in ends and block lightly.

state of mind

by veera välimäki

Sometimes it's hard to see beyond the hasty thoughts of your mind. This lovely cardigan, worked in one piece from top down, will keep your attention and makes it easy to shift your focus. Quiet your mind with this charming sweater and with its classic cables.

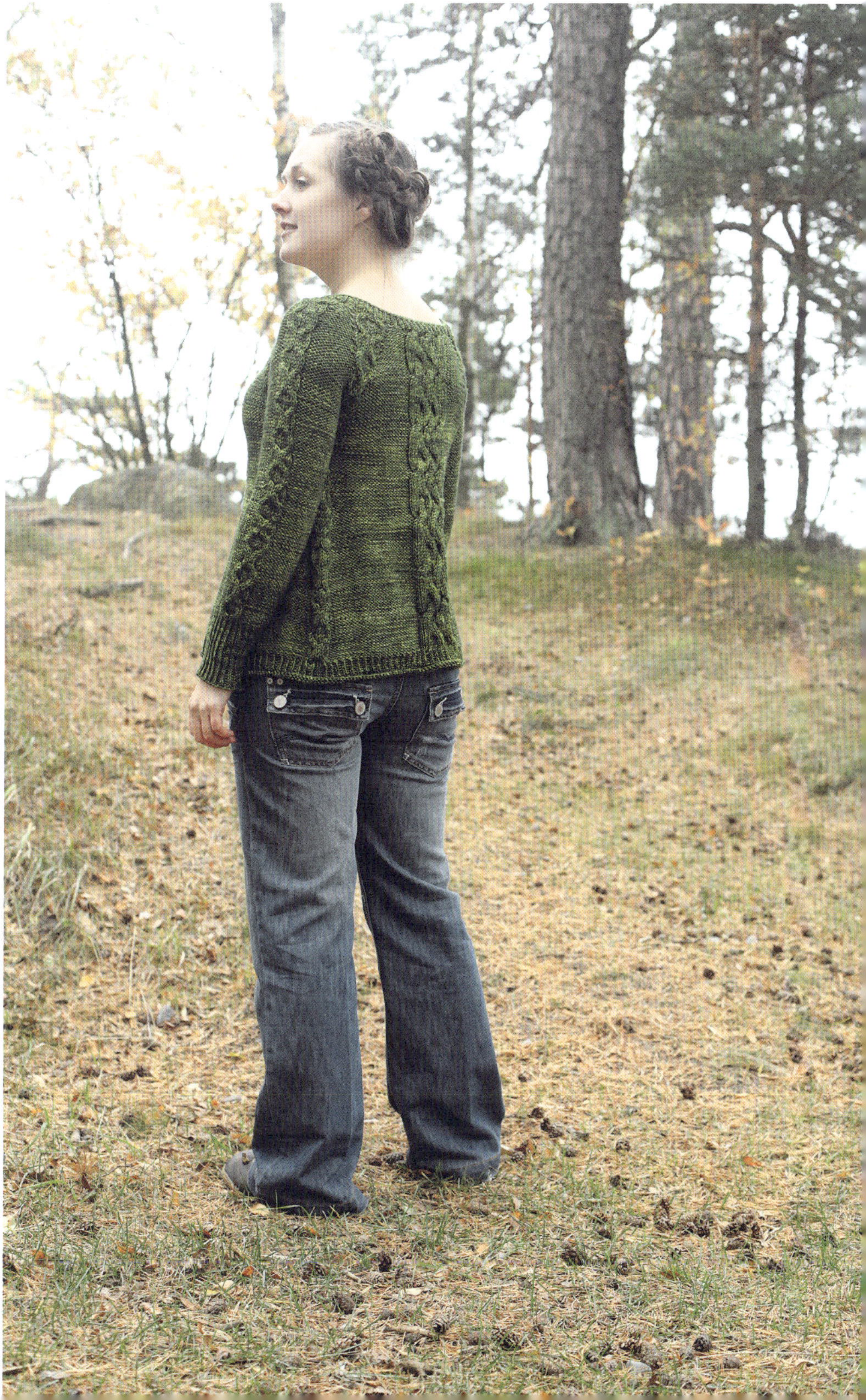

state of mind

Sizes

XS *(S, M, L, XL, XXL)*, shown in size S.
Finished chest circumference: 30 (34, 38, 42, 46, 50)" [75 (85, 95, 105, 115, 125) cm]. Choose the size with no ease or a bit of positive ease.

Materials

Yarn: 5 (5, 6, 6, 7, 8) skeins of Tosh Vintage by Madelinetosh (100% merino; 200 yd [182 m] - 100 g). Approx. 900 (980, 1080, 1200, 1350, 1470) yd [820 (900, 990, 1080, 1230, 1340) m] of worsted weight yarn. The sample was knit in colorway Jade.

Needles: US 8 [5 mm] and US 7 [4.5 mm] circular needle - 28" [80 cm] long, and dpns. Adjust needle size if necessary to obtain the correct gauge.

Other: Four 1¼" [3 cm] buttons, stitch markers, stitch holders / waste yarn, tapestry needle, and blocking aids.

Gauge

18 stitches and 32 rows = 4" [10 cm] in reverse Stockinette stitch using larger needle, after blocking.

Finished Measurements

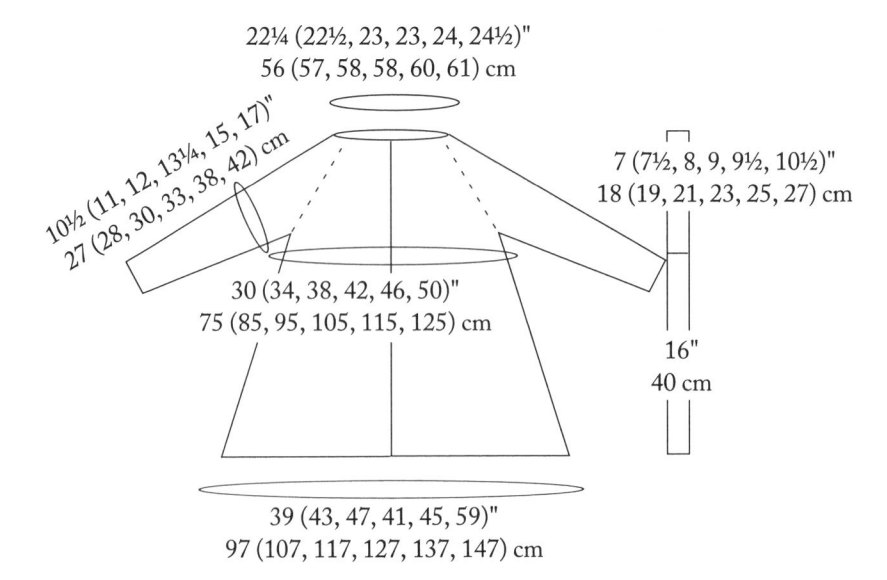

22¼ (22½, 23, 23, 24, 24½)"
56 (57, 58, 58, 60, 61) cm

10½ (11, 12, 13¼, 15, 17)"
27 (28, 30, 33, 38, 42) cm

7 (7½, 8, 9, 9½, 10½)"
18 (19, 21, 23, 25, 27) cm

30 (34, 38, 42, 46, 50)"
75 (85, 95, 105, 115, 125) cm

16"
40 cm

39 (43, 47, 41, 45, 59)"
97 (107, 117, 127, 137, 147) cm

state of mind

Collar

Using smaller circular needle, CO 110 (112, 114, 114, 118, 120) stitches. Do not join. Knit one row (RS) and work 3 rows in twisted ribbing (*WS: *k1, p1 tbl; rep from *; RS: *k1 tbl, p1; rep from **). Work the first buttonhole on next row (RS): Work in twisted ribbing until 6 sts remain, k2tog tbl, yo, work to end in twisted ribbing. Work 3 more rounds in twisted ribbing.

Yoke

Change to larger circular needle and begin raglan increases and cable patterns. *Note: See charts on page 99. You can add markers of each side of the cables if that makes it easier to distinguish them. Also, there will be no more buttonholes, because the holes formed by cable twists are used as buttonholes.*

Row 1 (RS, set-up row): Work row 1 of chart A once, p1, work row 1 of chart A once, purl 0 (1, 2, 2, 3, 4), m1Rp, work row 1 of chart A once, m1Lp, purl 2 (1, 0, 0, 0, 0), work row 1 of chart A once, purl 2 (1, 0, 0, 0, 0), m1Rp, work row 1 of chart A once, m1Lp, purl 1 (3, 5, 5, 6, 7), work row 1 of chart B, purl 1 (3, 5, 5, 6, 7), m1Rp, work row 1 of chart A once, m1Lp, purl 2 (1, 0, 0, 0, 0), work row 1 of chart A once, purl 2 (1, 0, 0, 0, 0), m1Rp, work row 1 of chart A once, m1Lp, purl 0 (1, 2, 2, 3, 4), work row 1 of chart A once, p1, work row 1 of chart A once more to end.

Row 2 (WS): Work row 2 of chart A, k1, work row 2 of chart A, knit to next cable, work row 2 of chart A, knit to next cable, work row 2 of chart A, knit to next cable, work row 2 of chart A, knit to next cable, work row 2 of chart B, knit to next cable, work row 2 of chart A, knit to next cable, work row 2 of chart A, knit to next cable, work row 2 of chart A, knit to next cable, work row 2 of chart A, k1, work row 2 of chart A to end.

Row 3 (RS): Work the next row of chart A, p1, work the next row of chart A, purl to next cable, m1Rp, work the next row of chart A, m1Lp, purl to next cable, work the next row of chart A, purl to next cable, m1Rp, work the next row of chart A, m1Lp, purl to next cable, work the next row of chart B, purl to next cable, m1Rp, work the next row of chart A, m1Lp, purl to next cable, work the next row of chart A, purl to next cable, m1Rp, work the next row of chart A, m1Lp, purl to next cable, work the next row of chart A, p1, work the next row of chart A to end.

Row 4 (WS): Work the next row of chart A, k1, work the next row of chart A, knit to next cable, work the next row of chart A, knit to next cable, work the next row of chart A, knit to next cable, work the next row of chart A, knit to next cable, work the next row of chart B, knit to next cable, work the next row of chart A, knit to next cable, work the next row of chart A, knit to next cable, work the next row of chart A, knit to next cable, work the next row of chart A, k1, work the next row of chart A to end.

Repeat *rows 3 and 4* – 14 (16, 19, 23, 26, 29) more times [*238 (256, 282, 314, 342, 368) stitches on needle*].

Divide for body and sleeves

Next row (RS): Work the next row of chart A, p1, work the next row of chart A, purl to next cable, work the next row of chart A, place the next 44 (46, 50, 58, 64, 70) stitches on holder for sleeve, CO 1 (1, 1, 1, 2, 4) stitches using backwards loop cast-on, work the next row of chart A, purl to next cable, work the next row of chart B, purl to next cable, work the next row of chart A, place the next 44 (46, 50, 58, 64, 70) stitches on holder for sleeve, CO 1 (1, 1, 1, 2, 4) stitches using backwards loop cast-on, work the next row of chart A, purl to next cable, work the next row of chart A, p1, work the next row of chart A.

You now have 152 (166, 184, 200, 218, 236) stitches on needle for the body and 44 (46, 50, 58, 64, 70) stitches on each holder for sleeves.

Body

Continue working back and forth in reverse Stockinette and cable patterns -

Row 5 (RS): Work the next row of chart A, p1, work the next row of chart A, purl to next cable, work the next row of chart A, purl to next cable, work the next row of chart B, purl to next cable, work the next row of chart A, purl to next cable, work the next row of chart A, purl to next cable, work the next row of chart A, p1, work the next row of chart A to end.

Row 6 (WS): Work the next row of chart A, k1, work the next row of chart A, knit to next cable, work the next row of chart A, knit to next cable, work the next row of chart A, knit to next cable, work the next row of chart B, knit to next cable, work the next row of chart A, knit to next cable, work the next row of chart A, knit to next cable, work the next row of chart A, k1, work the next row of chart A to end.

Repeat *rows 5 and 6* until the body measures 3" [8 cm] from underarm. Begin A-line shaping.

Row 7 (RS): Work the next row of chart A, p1, work the next row of chart A, purl to next cable, work the next row of chart A, m1Lp, purl to next cable, m1Rp, work the next row of chart A, purl to next cable, work the next row of chart B, purl to next cable, work the next row of chart A, m1Lp, purl to next cable, m1Rp, work the next row of chart A, purl to next cable, work the next row of chart A, p1, work the next row of chart A to end.

Row 8 (WS): Work the next row of chart A, k1, work the next row of chart A, knit to next cable, work the next row of chart A, knit to next cable, work the next row of chart A, knit to next cable, work the next row of chart B, knit to next cable, work the next row of chart A, knit to next cable, work the next row of chart A, knit to next cable, work the next row of chart A, k1, work the next row of chart A to end.

Repeat *rows 5 to 8* – 9 more times [*40 stitches increased; 192 (206, 224, 240, 258, 276) stitches on needle*].

Continue even as established, repeating rows 5 and 6 (no more side increases), until the body measures 15" [38 cm] from underarm. Change to smaller circular needle and work 6 rounds in twisted ribbing (*WS: *k1, p1 tbl; rep from *; RS: *k1 tbl, p1; rep from **). Work two rows in Stockinette stitch and BO body stitches on next row (RS).

Sleeves

Note: you can pick up a few extra stitches from the underarm if desired, but decrease these extra stitches on next possible round.

Place the held stitches on larger dpns. Starting at the center of underarm, pick up and purl 2 stitches, work the stitches on needles (purl to cable, work the next row of chart A, purl to under arm) and pick up and purl 2 stitches to end. Place marker to indicate the beginning of the round and join. Work in rev St st and continue cable pattern as established for 4" [10 cm], then begin sleeve decreases.

Decrease round (RS): Purl 2, p2tog, work as established until 4 stitches remain, ssp, purl 2.

Repeat the *decrease round* 3 more times every 2" [5 cm]. Continue working in rev St st and cable A as established until the sleeve measures 15" [38 cm].

Change to smaller dpns and continue in twisted ribbing (*k1 tbl, p1; rep from * to end*). Work 4" [10 cm] in twisted ribbing and then knit 2 rounds. BO sleeve stitches loosely.

Finishing

Weave in ends and block garment to finished measurements.

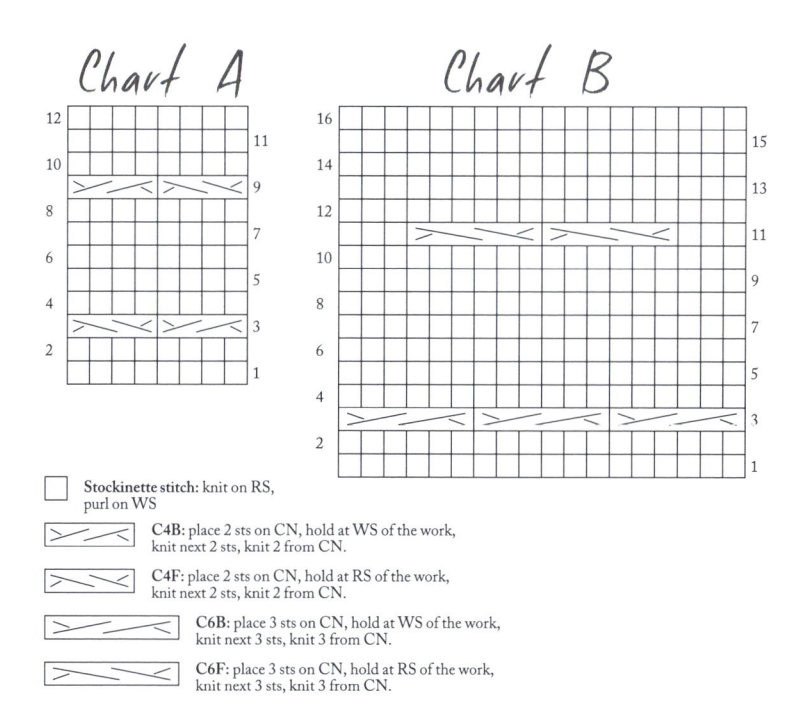

Chart A

Chart B

Stockinette stitch: knit on RS, purl on WS

C4B: place 2 sts on CN, hold at WS of the work, knit next 2 sts, knit 2 from CN.

C4F: place 2 sts on CN, hold at RS of the work, knit next 2 sts, knit 2 from CN.

C6B: place 3 sts on CN, hold at WS of the work, knit next 3 sts, knit 3 from CN.

C6F: place 3 sts on CN, hold at RS of the work, knit next 3 sts, knit 3 from CN.

glossary

glossary of terms and useful links

Wrap and Turn

A great tutorial by The Purl Bee on short rows can be found here:
http://www.purlbee.com/2008/06/18/short-rows/

Provisional cast on

I use the crochet provisional cast on. There is a great tutorial by Lucy Neatby on Youtube. I find it extremely clear and I love to use this technique because I end up will all my provisional stitches on the needle:
http://www.youtube.com/watch?v=R3J-sUx_whE

Elastic Bind-Off

Knit 1, *knit next st, insert left needle through the front loops of both st on your right needle and knit them together through the back loop*, repeat to the end of row.

abbreviations

approx:	Approximately
BO:	Bind Off
CC:	Contrasting Color
C4B:	Place 2 sts on CN, hold at WS of the work, knit next 2 sts, knit 2 from CN.
C4F:	Place 2 sts on CN, hold at RS of the work, knit next 2 sts, knit 2 from CN.
C6B:	Place 3 sts on CN, hold at WS of the work, knit next 3 sts, knit 3 from CN.
C6F:	Place 3 sts on CN, hold at RS of the work, knit next 3 sts, knit 3 from CN.
CO:	Cast On
foll(s):	Follows, following
Garter st:	Garter stitch; Back and forth: knit on RS and WS; In the round: knit one round; purl one round.
k:	Knit
k1fb:	Knit into front of the stitch, leave stitch on left needle and knit into back of the same stitch; increase.
k2tog:	Knit 2 sts together; decrease.
m:	marker
MC:	Main Color
MB:	Make Bobble: Kfbf (knit through the front, back, and then front again) into the same st, turn work. P3, turn work K3. Slip 2nd and 3rd st on the RN, one by one, over the 1st one.
m1p:	Purled increase. With left needle tip, lift strand between needles, from back to front. Purl lifted loop.
m1Rp:	Right slanting increase, make one right; pick up the strand between the stitches from back, purl through the front of the stitch.
m1Lp:	Left slanting increase, make one left; pick up the strand between the stitches from front, purl through the back of the stitch.
m1L:	Increase slanted to the left (pick up the horizontal bar btw the sts from front to back, knit through back leg).
m1R:	Increase slanted to the right (pick up the horizontal bar btw the sts from back to front, knit through front leg).
patt:	Pattern
pm:	Place marker
p:	Purl
p1fb:	Purl into front of the stitch, leave stitch on left needle and purl into back of the same stitch; increase.
p2tog:	Purl 2 sts together; decrease.
RS:	Right side
rev St st:	Reverse Stockinette stitch; knit on WS, purl on RS.
sk2p:	Sl 1, k2 as if to k2tog, pass slipped st over.
sl:	Slip
sm:	Slip marker
ssk:	Slip, slip, knit slipped sts tbl; decrease.
ssp:	Slip, slip, purl slipped sts tbl; decrease.
st(s):	Stitch (stitches)
St st:	Stockinette stitch; knit on RS, purl on WS.
tbl:	Through back loop
tog:	Together
WS:	Wrong side
W&T:	Wrap and turn; work to place stated in pattern, bring yarn front, slip the next st without knitting it, bring the yarn back, slide the slipped st back on left needle, and turn work.
yo:	Yarn over

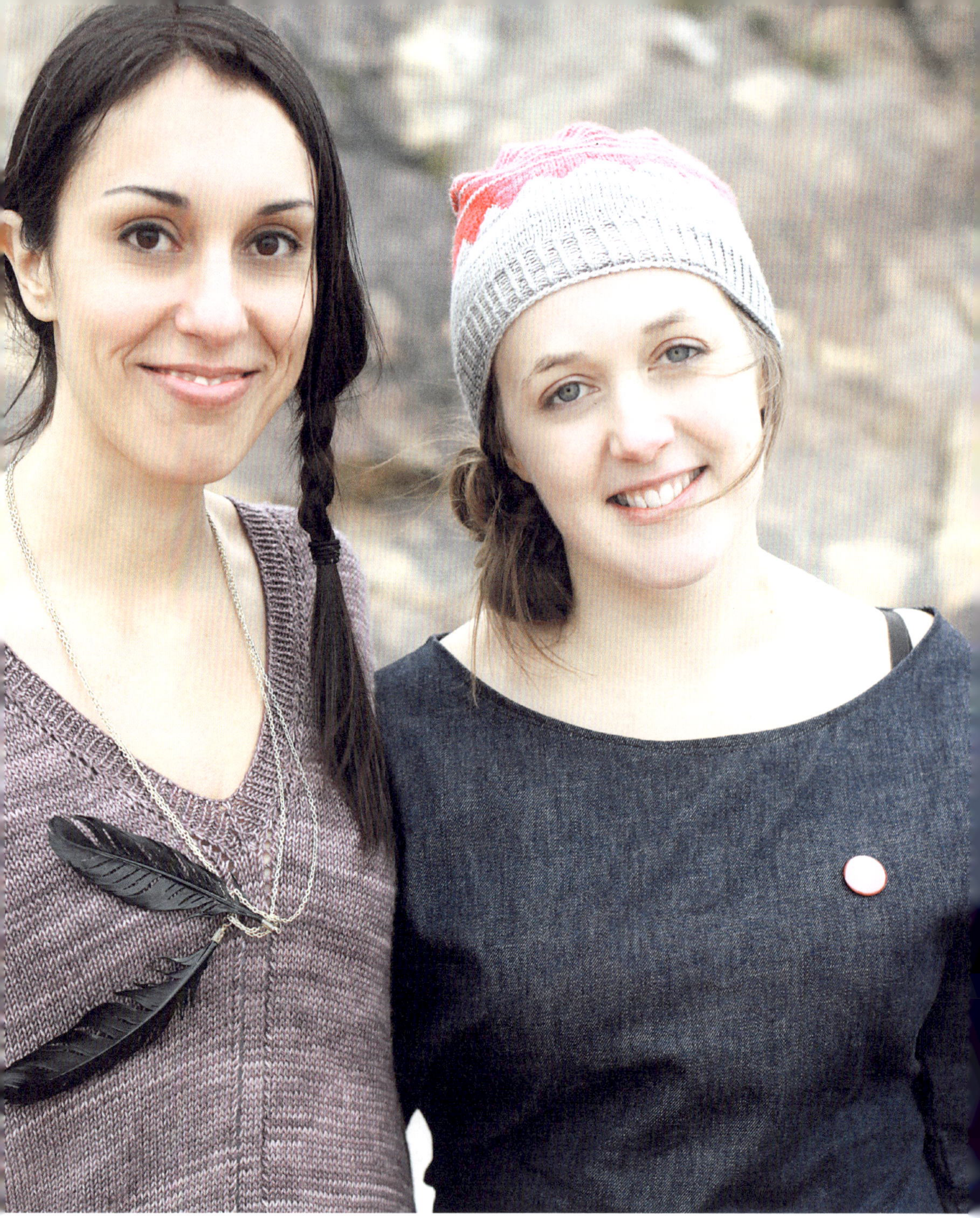